AIR CAMPAIGN

GOTHIC LINE 1944–45
The USAAF starves out the German Army

THOMAS McKELVEY CLEAVER

ILLUSTRATED BY ANASTASIOS
POLYCHRONIS

Author's acknowledgments

This book could not have been written
without the involvement of the originals
– the men who flew these missions. I met
them just in time, as within four years of
writing my first book on the 57th Bomb
Wing, they had all departed.

Dan Bowling, who was gone three
months after I interviewed him, was one
of the most outstanding of the World War
II originals I have ever met over a 40-year
career. His good friend, Paul Jackson, was
right when he described Dan thus: "He
was the squadron leader; that's different
from being the squadron commander."
Dan's book, *Follow PDI*, which he wrote
after he returned home from the war, was
devastating in its honesty and written in
the white heat of personal feeling. It was
a "time machine" to interview the young
flyer who had experienced all those things.

Paul Jackson, who was my original
"door" into the story spent 70 years saying
nothing until his daughter got him to go
to a bomb wing reunion. When I was able
to talk to him, the memories flooded out
in honesty and passion. When he talked
of those who I couldn't interview, his
memories were so strong that I came away
feeling I did know those others.

Sterling Ditchey, who navigated
12,000 miles across the planet with "three
maps, a protractor, and four pencils"
a month after he turned 20, had kept
everything from those days and was a
gold mine of information. He died ten
days before his friend George Underwood
joined him in 2020. Both of them "put
me in the airplane" with their memories.

And finally my collaborator on this
book, Dan Setzer, the man who really
"saved everything" about the 57th Bomb
Wing. None of this could have been done
without his passion to keep the history
alive.

It's been the privilege of my writing
career to finally tell the real story of the
men who spent their lives in the shadow
of "Catch-22."

Thomas McKelvey Cleaver
Encino, California, 2021

Meet me over Rovereto
Meet me in the air
There ain't no place
The flak is thicker
No place else but there
We will take evasive action
They will miss us by a fraction
So meet me over Rovereto
Meet me in the air
Aircrew Song (1944)
(Sung to "Meet Me in St. Louis")

CONTENTS

INTRODUCTION

The Allies invading Salerno. The MP (Military Policeman) in the foreground ducks when a blast from an 88mm round explodes nearby. (NARA)

Following the successful conclusion of the Allied campaign in Sicily, which reopened the sea lanes in the Mediterranean between Gibraltar and Egypt, the Allied leaders were once again at loggerheads over what should be the next move against the Axis powers. Only one Allied leader voiced his desire to engage in further campaigns in the Mediterranean: Prime Minister Winston Churchill believed a campaign to liberate Italy would allow the Western Allied armies to move into the Balkans and Eastern Europe ahead of the Soviets. The American military leadership was firmly opposed to such a campaign, seeing rightly that any such action was a distraction from the main event: the defeat of Hitler's Germany. They argued that while an Italian campaign might force the Germans to spread their forces and turn some attention away from northwestern Europe, nothing that happened in Italy would have any impact on the outcome of the central confrontation across the old Western Front. Indeed, American leaders had only been persuaded to engage the enemy in North Africa because of President Roosevelt's domestic political need for an offensive action in Europe at the earliest moment.

The Sicilian campaign had been opposed by American leaders, who wanted a cross-Channel invasion in 1943. However, the fact that this was impossible due to a shortage of landing craft that would not be met until 1944 had allowed Churchill to successfully press for an invasion of Sicily, which he claimed would put pressure on Italy to quit the war. With Sicily under Allied control and the shortage of invasion craft still unresolved, the prime minister argued that failing to undertake another campaign before the cross-Channel invasion would give the Germans breathing space to reorganize their forces and perhaps create a defense in northern France that the Allies could not break, while lack of fighting would demoralize the home front without news of continued victories. Once Churchill definitely committed himself to supporting an invasion of northern France in 1944, Roosevelt agreed to support further military effort in Italy. Again, expediency ruled the day.

Germany decides to defend in Italy

Churchill had been right that invading Sicily would put pressure on the Italians to withdraw from the war. Throughout July 1943, anti-Mussolini factions in the government in Rome had worked to rid themselves of the dictator, and Il Duce had been forced to resign as prime minister on July 25. Marshal Badoglio assumed leadership, charged by King Victor Emmanuel III with finding a way to make peace. On September 3, 1943, the Armistice of Cassibile saw Italy surrender and pledge to join the fight against Germany. At the same time, the British Eighth Army crossed the Straits of Messina in Operation *Baytown* without casualties, the Italian government having ordered their armed forces not to resist.

With Mussolini's arrest, the Germans planned to occupy the country should the government surrender. Surprisingly, Hitler supported such an occupation in his belief that the Allies' ultimate goal involved invading southern Italy to gain control of the airfields around Foggia, then to use these and airfields on Sicily to support an invasion of Greece and the Balkans. He understood Churchill's desire to move into Eastern Europe and forestall the Soviets, and knew that since his allies in Bulgaria, Romania, and Hungary were not strongly committed to the Axis cause, it might not be such a difficult move.

The leaders of the US Army were not the only ones to look askance at a war in Italy. Following the Axis surrender in North Africa, Field Marshal Erwin Rommel arrived in Italy to take command of Army Group B, which would be responsible for occupying all of the country in the event of a surrender. Hitler promised Rommel six infantry and *Panzergrenadier* (mechanized infantry) divisions, two Panzer divisions, and two divisions of Luftwaffe paratroops that would be transferred from France, with two additional Panzer divisions from the Eastern Front. As it happened, the scale of the German tank losses in the enormous armored battle at Kursk in July 1943 precluded the transfer of the two Eastern Front divisions.

Rommel, reporting to Hitler that Italy could not be defended without the cooperation of the Italian Army, advocated that a defensive line be created south of the Po Valley in the northern Apennine mountains, capable of blocking an attempt by the Allies to enter the Reich through the south.

There was one other man besides Churchill who advocated a fight on the Italian peninsula. Luftwaffe Field Marshal Albert Kesselring – commander-in-chief of German forces on the Southern Front, which included Italy – had long believed an Allied invasion was inevitable. He planned a full-on defense, using the German units that had been held back in Italy when the Afrika Korps surrendered in May, as well as the Italian Army, which he predicted would remain loyal. Marshal Kesselring believed Hitler favored Rommel's plan, and when paratroop commander General Kurt Student arrived to plan a possible *coup d'état* in Rome to arrest the king and Badoglio, Kesselring presented detailed plans for such a defense. He stated his belief that Rome could be held until the summer of 1944 if he were allowed to wage a campaign of attrition, forcing the Allies to pay in blood for every inch of territory taken in Calabria and Apulia, and delaying their advance as long as possible. He also stated flatly that the Allies would not invade beyond the range of their air cover on Sicily, correctly naming Salerno as the most likely invasion target and advocating that German forces occupy the region and fortify against such a move.

General Sir Harold Alexander (left) with Major General Lucian K Truscott Jr (right) at Anzio, March 4, 1944. (IWM/Getty Images)

Kesselring presciently stated that after Rome fell the next summer, the army should then retreat north and take up a position in the line of fortifications Rommel had named "the Hitler Line," where they could hold out "indefinitely" so long as sufficient supplies could be secured through the Brenner Pass linking Italy with Austria. Student was impressed by Kesselring's presentation and reported it to Hitler. When he visited his generals again in early September, Hitler listened to Kesselring, who had taken responsibility to move units of the Tenth Army into position around Salerno, but he directed Rommel to continue building what had been prudently renamed the "Gothic Line" to avoid the possibility of incurring Hitler's rage should the operation fail. Rumors began to swirl on September 7 that the Italian surrender would become effective the next day. On the evening of September 8, Kesselring bowed to the inevitable and ordered his forces to prepare to evacuate if the order was given, but to hold their positions until they received the withdrawal order.

The Allies invade

The Allies had only decided to land on the Italian mainland in late July and suffered from an intelligence disadvantage, since all German communications were by landline rather than radio, shielding them from Ultra codebreaking. Some planners advocated a *coup de main*, dropping paratroops into Rome on September 8 to coincide with the surrender, coupled with landing the main force on the coast at Nettuno to cut off the enemy army in southern Italy. This plan was dropped when it became clear that there was no way to provide aerial support beyond the range of air forces in Sicily. Planning then focused on Salerno, the northernmost possibility, as Kesselring had predicted. The hope of an airborne landing continued, with General Maxwell Taylor of the 82nd Airborne Division landing secretly at Anzio in early September to meet with the Italian authorities in Rome to plan the event. In the end, the Italians could not promise loyal army units to support the Americans, while it also became obvious that Kesselring's forces in the city were far more active than had been expected. The coming campaign would thus see no audacious Allied strategy.

The British Eighth Army landed at Taranto on September 8. There was no opposition, since Kesselring did not see this as being the main attack. He ordered the activation of Operation *Achse* to disarm Italian units and occupy important positions. Rommel disarmed the northern units, while Kesselring ordered those in the south to go home. By September 15, the Italian Army had disappeared, leaving the Wehrmacht in full control of further war in the peninsula. Had the Allies waited until September 12, the date the Italians expected the invasion and that the Germans were using to coordinate plans for their withdrawal to Rome, Hitler's order to evacuate German forces in southern Italy would not have been given until September 9 and the invasion would have found the German Tenth Army in the midst of withdrawal, which would have prevented opposition to the invading Allies. Now, in the face of the Allied landing, with the Tenth Army still in southern Italy,

The bombed-out shell of the monastery at Monte Cassino. The 340th Bomb Group was first in to bomb the abbey, but the newspapers at home gave all the credit to the B-17s. Warning was given and the monastery was evacuated, the artwork removed. The Allies targeted the monastery because they were convinced that the Germans were using it for military purposes. They weren't. (Photo by Keystone-France/Gamma-Rapho via Getty Images)

In addition to danger in the air, there was also danger on the ground. This photo shows a Ju-87 Stuka dive-bomber given to the Italian Regia Aeronautica (as identified by the Italian insignia on the tail) at Catania, Sicily, in December 1943. The hole just forward of the cockpit is the result of the detonation of a booby trap set by the retreating forces. (57th Bomb Wing Archives, Edward Betts Collection)

force majeure required that a stand be made, and the Wehrmacht thus stood firm in the south of the peninsula.

Operation *Avalanche* on September 9, which saw the US Fifth Army and elements of the British Eighth Army and the Canadian Army come ashore at Salerno, was the main attack Kesselring anticipated. To maximize surprise, invasion commander Lt General Mark W. Clark had foregone the traditional preliminary air and naval bombardment. Yet there was no surprise; the Germans were ready and able to respond. As the first wave of the American 36th (Texas) Infantry Division approached the shore at Paestum, a loudspeaker in the landing area proclaimed in English: "Come on in and give up. We have you covered." The first wave landed into the teeth of the four battle groups of the 16th Panzer Division. By the end of the day, lead Allied elements could look down on the plain of Naples but were hard-pressed to keep their position.

That night, the Hermann Göring and 15th Panzergrenadier divisions moved to the battlefield. Fighting was intense during the next three days as Kesselring fed in more units while Allied reinforcements were constrained by limited transport availability and the predetermined build-up schedule. Kesselring asked Rommel to send him the two Army Group B Panzer divisions, but Rommel refused on the grounds that their loss could not be risked if he was to successfully defend northern Italy after Kesselring's forces were defeated. After the war, Kesselring told his Allied interrogators he believed that if Rommel had sent him the two armored divisions by September 13, he could have defeated the Salerno invasion. Considering how hard the fighting was, two experienced armored divisions might well have tipped the balance in the Germans' favor.

As it was, the Allies were forced to drop the 82nd Airborne Division on the invasion beaches to provide reinforcement when the German counterattack came on September 13. Two German battle groups overran two battalions of the 36th Infantry Division and nearly wiped them out. They were only stopped by US artillery firing over open sights, naval gunfire, and a makeshift position manned and held by artillerymen, drivers, cooks, and clerks. At one point, General Clark seriously considered the possibility of an evacuation under fire.

The German attacks were repulsed with heavy casualties the next day. That night, every Allied bomber in North Africa and Sicily hit enemy positions in the surrounding hills. Next day, the Hermann Göring Division's attack was stopped by naval gunfire, including the 15in guns of HMS *Warspite*.

Hitler was impressed with the results and agreed with Kesselring on September 15 that a delayed withdrawal was correct. Kesselring ordered the preparation of a defensive line on the Volturno and Rapido rivers north of Naples, which he called the Bernhard Line. On September 16, the Luftwaffe used Fritz-X guided bombs against the invasion fleet, damaging HMS *Warspite* and sinking two cargo ships.

The battle of attrition

Beginning on September 17, the German Tenth Army under General Heinrich von Vietinghof began a fighting withdrawal which extended over the next month until his troops occupied the Bernhard defenses from which they would block any further American advance. Von Vietinghof had come within an ace of defeating the Salerno beachhead and would continue to stymie his opponents over the next 18 months. American planners had not anticipated such resistance; it was a failure of imagination and planning that would repeat itself in the months to come.

On September 19, the Allies attacked toward Naples and the freshly landed US 3rd Infantry Division, commanded by Major General Lucian K. Truscott, Jr, took Acerno, followed by the liberation of Avellino on September 28. The following day, the Eighth Army captured the major airfield complex at Foggia which would become the primary base of Allied airpower. On October 1, Allied forces entered Naples following the German withdrawal in the face of rebellion by the people of the city.

Hitler summoned Kesselring and Rommel to his headquarters on October 4 to hear their views on a counteroffensive. Rommel, overestimating Allied amphibious capability, believed a line too far south was a great danger, though he admitted to hold the Bernhard Line it would take half the divisions necessary to defend his line in the Appenines. Rommel's negative attitude toward fighting in the south convinced Hitler he was no longer reliable. Kesselring was ordered to finish the Bernhard Line, though Hitler did not completely accept Kesselring's optimism about being able to hold the Allies in the south for six to nine months, and also ordered Rommel to complete the Gothic Line. He then appointed Kesselring Commander-in-Chief Southwest (i.e., the Italian theater) and

The future General Knapp (3rd from the left, front row) during pilot training in 1928 at Baker Field. Robert Knapp was a respected leader of the 57th Bomb Wing, and a pioneer of military aviation. He was an early advocate of the radar-controlled SHORAN bombing technology. (57th Bomb Wing Archives)

Army Group C. The Luftwaffe field marshal had won a major victory in the argument to define the rest of the war in Italy. On November 21, Rommel was sent to France to finish the Atlantic Wall. After Kesselring, the two main impediments to Allied success would be the pedestrian British General Sir Harold Alexander, a Churchill favorite in overall theater command, and General Mark Clark, whose lust for glory would lengthen the battle in Italy by nearly a year.

The Salerno bloodbath was only a taste of what was to come. By mid-October, the Germans were safely in the Bernhard Line; further north, the Gustav Line, centered on Monte Cassino and blocking the advance to Rome, was completed. The Bernhard Line held the Allies following the rains of November and the blizzards and drifting snow of December.

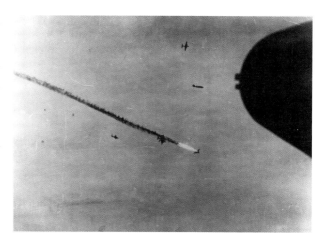

8H was shot down on February 16, 1944, over Campoleone, supporting the invasion at Anzio. A direct hit set the engine on fire. Only the navigator, Sgt Mones E. Hawley, was able to bail out. He was captured immediately by the Germans. (57th Bomb Wing Archives)

In January 1944, General Dwight D. Eisenhower, Allied commander since the North African invasion, left to become Supreme Commander, Allied Expeditionary Forces for the forthcoming Normandy invasion. He took with him the US 1st Infantry Division, "The Big Red One," which had proven its worth and reputation in North Africa, Sicily, and Italy, as well as the 82nd Airborne, the most experienced American paratroop division with drops at Casablanca, Sicily, and Salerno. Allied forces in Italy would find themselves progressively weaker against their German opponents as men, materiel, and equipment were diverted to operations aimed more directly at German defeat. No other Allied campaign in Europe was more costly in lives lost and wounds suffered by infantrymen than the bitter small-scale fights at the Bernhard Line, the Gustav Line, Anzio, and the Gothic Line. In the end, the war in Italy was fought because it was there.

General Clark's mistake

Shortly after Eisenhower's departure, Fifth Army reached the Gustav Line on January 15, following six weeks of heavy fighting to break through the Bernhardt Line, during which the Allied armies suffered 16,000 casualties; Kesselring's strategy of making the Allies pay in blood for every foot of Italy they took was bearing fruit. On January 22, General Truscott's new command, VI Corps, attempted an "end run" around the Gustav Line by landing at Anzio, but indecisive American frontline leadership allowed the Wehrmacht's Fourteenth Army to surround the beachhead, turning it into a "meatgrinder" for Truscott's force.

Between January 20 and May 11, four attempts to break the Gustav Line would see the aerial destruction of the medieval monastery and some of the worst Allied casualties of the entire war before the Polish division finally fought its way to the crest of Cassino on May 12. Three days later, Commonwealth units had moved into positions from where they could cut off the German Tenth Army from its path to Rome. At this point, there was reason for optimism that the Italian campaign would soon end.

The Allied plan involved a breakout from Anzio by Truscott's VI Corps when the German retreat from the Gustav Line began, heading southeast to connect with Canadian Army forces and "bag" the Tenth Army. Unfortunately, General Clark's ego intervened. Desperate for the glory of being the liberator of Rome, Clark had actually asked Eisenhower to delay *Overlord* – the invasion of northern France – for two weeks to allow time to celebrate the fall of Rome. When Truscott's troops were successful in their breakout, Clark ordered him to turn northeast instead and liberate the Eternal City.

General Mark Clark, who wanted the glory of being the "Liberator of Rome." To achieve that, he allowed the German Tenth Army to escape a trap as they retreated from Monte Cassino. Two days after Rome was liberated, the D-Day invasion of France totally overshadowed the liberation of Rome, robbing Clark of the glory he sought. (Photo by Keystone/Getty Images)

The Germans escape to the Gothic Line

The Tenth Army found the gap between US VI Corps' southern flank and the Canadians, and the Germans made a successful forced march north. While American troops liberated Rome – which had fallen without a fight when the Germans withdrew – Tenth Army marched around the city and linked up with the Fourteenth Army as it withdrew from the Anzio fighting.

Immediately after the victory at Cassino and the fall of Rome, General Truscott's VI Corps and the French Expeditionary Corps – a total of seven combat-hardened experienced divisions – were withdrawn from operations in Italy to participate in Operation *Dragoon*, the Allied invasion of southern France on August 17, 1944.

Over the course of the summer of 1944, a series of pitched battles were fought in Italy as the Allies kept up pressure on the retreating Germans. The fighting retreat of the Tenth and Fourteenth armies was a masterful display of generalship on the part of Kesselring and his field commander, von Vietinghoff. Their forces held the Allies at each position to the last moment, withdrawing just in time to avoid destruction and leaving their opponents with growing frustration.

Operation *Strangle*

Throughout the Italian campaign, the USAAF 12 Air Force was committed to Operation *Strangle*, a plan to cut off the German retreat first at the Bernhard Line and later at the Gustav Line, through bombing of the Italian transportation system, concentrating on bridges. Bridges are notoriously difficult targets for bombers; destruction of the span itself does not necessarily mean the crossing will be abandoned unless the approaches on either side are also destroyed, since otherwise the enemy can construct pontoon bridges and other temporary structures. Defense against the bombers is simplified by the fact that the main route of attack is obvious, making the siting of antiaircraft weapons considerably more straightforward.

Another bridge over the Po River goes down. Note the number of bomb craters, indicating multiple visits to this target. The bombers flew in very close formation to ensure that the bombs would all land in a tight pattern on the target. (57th Bomb Wing Archives)

"The Bridgebusters"

Throughout this aerial campaign, four B-25 bomb groups – which were combined in January 1944 into the 57th Bomb Wing – had been in the forefront of the air support campaign.

The 321st Bomb Group had arrived in the Mediterranean Theater of Operations (MTO) in February 1943. The unit was commanded by Colonel Robert D. Knapp, a man with a lifelong involvement in aviation since meeting the Wright Brothers at the age of ten when they stayed with his family for ten days in 1907. Commissioned a 2nd lieutenant in the Air Service in March 1918, he held US Pilot License Number 187, signed by Orville Wright, and had been flying for longer than most of his young aircrews had been alive. In 1919, he served on the US–Mexico border with future USAAF leaders Hap Arnold and Ira Eaker. In 1923, he pioneered the air mail route from Montgomery, Alabama, to New Orleans. Made Chief of Primary Flight Training at Randolph and Kelly fields in 1929, he was responsible for all Air Corps flight training. In 1937, he led a 98-plane formation on a national tour to recruit ROTC (Reserve Officers' Training Corps) students at land-grant colleges into aviation in anticipation of a future buildup of the corps.

The effect of accurate bombing on bridges could be catastrophic. Bridges over large expanses like the Po River were put out of commission for the duration. Smaller bridges like those in the Brenner Pass were quickly rebuilt or diversions constructed, causing US bombers to return again and again to the same targets. (57th Bomb Wing Archives, Edward Betts Collection)

OPPOSITE USS *CORSICA*, THE UNSINKABLE ISLAND AIRCRAFT CARRIER

When war preparation began in 1941, Knapp organized the first six B-25 bomb groups, and personally trained three: the 310th, 321st, and 340th groups – units that would form his future command. After much "politicking," he was able to take the 321st Group to North Africa, despite being considered too old for direct combat duty. Having trained the crews who had gone on to take part in the Doolittle Raid on Tokyo, he was able to get several of the survivors assigned to the three groups, giving the new aircrews experienced role models.

At the age of 45, Knapp took the 321st through the North African, Sicilian, and Balkans campaigns, personally leading 40 tough missions, including the first bombing of Rome. He was awarded the Silver Star for a successful unescorted raid on an Axis convoy, and the 321st received its first Presidential Unit Citation for the attack on Athens in September 1943. Knapp was promoted to brigadier general and became commander of the 57th Bomb Wing when it was formed in January 1944 to bring the three groups under a central command. Later caricatured as "General Dreedle" in the novel *Catch 22* by Joseph Heller, those who trained under and served with him saw Dreedle's polar opposite: tough and demanding, never asking a man to do something he had not himself done first. The replacements who arrived in 1944 did not know the leader who always led "the tough ones." They knew him only as a hard taskmaster ordering them to fly mission after mission, unaware of his constant attempts to get timely replacements in sufficient numbers in the face of opposition by air forces "fighting the real war" over Germany.

The 310th Bomb Group had followed the 321st into North Africa in January 1943, and specialized in anti-shipping strikes following the German surrender in May. The 340th Bomb Group arrived in Egypt from India in the spring of 1943 and advanced west with the British forces. The 319th Bomb Group had arrived in North Africa just after the fighting at Kasserine Pass, and all four units had participated in the Pantelleria campaign – in which the Italian defenders surrendered in the face of air attacks before the planned invasion was mounted – and in the Sicilian campaign. Their initial operations in Italy had led Knapp to be able to successfully argue that the B-25 Mitchell units should be combined into their own command.

Many noted that food in the units of the 57th Bomb Wing was better than what was generally found in the Italian theater. This was because Knapp believed that good food was necessary for morale. Paul Young, a pilot with the 321st Group, remembered, "We flew regular 'rum runner' trips to Sicily for food and liquor, and even as far away as Tunisia or Egypt." Many of the young aircrew, for whom General Knapp was a distant figure, did not know he was the one who authorized the flights and the various business deals that filled their messes and clubs with luxuries. The 488th Bomb Squadron's War Diary noted one incident that showed what was going on: On September 16, 1944, 2nd Lt. Mauno A. Lindholm, the squadron 'mess officer' operating the rum runner flights for the 488th Bomb Squadron got caught trading coffee for fresh eggs in Catania by a British military police agent. The consequences of being caught could not have been too dire since Lindholm was piloting 8C over La Spezia only a week later. Knapp either interceded with the British or satisfied them by punishing Lindholm with a slap on the wrist. (Lindholm is considered by many to be the model for the character of Milo Minderbinder in *Catch-22*.)

Following the March 1944 eruption of Vesuvius that ruined the nearby airfields and destroyed more USAAF aircraft in two weeks than the Germans had accomplished in 18 months, the 57th Wing moved to newly liberated Corsica in late April 1944. The island, centrally located in the western Mediterranean in range of central and northern Italy, Austria, and southern France, became known as "USS Corsica, The Unsinkable Aircraft Carrier" that was home to American, Commonwealth, and Free French bomber and fighter squadrons.

Allied Air Base

Note: All Auxiliary Airfields were used during Operation *Dragoon*, the Allied invasion of Southern France.

Capraia

Elba

Pianosa

Monte Cristo

Bastia
Army Hospital

Bevinco
C-47 Army Supply

Calvi-Fiume Secco
Auxiliary Airfield, 52nd FG (RAF)

Sainte Catherine
Engineer Aviation Battalion

Calenzana
242 Fighter Squadron (RAF)

Borgo
3rd PRG, 111st TRS,
415th NFS, 2/33
(French Air Force)

Poretta
47th BG, 86th FG

Serraggia
27th FG, 79th FG

Alto
57th FG, 320th BG (B-26)

Cervione
Army Field Hospital

Corte
Piper Cub Landing Field

Alesani
340th BG

CORSICA

Aghione
52nd FG, 1st FG, 14th FG

Casabianda
USAAF C-47's Intelligence Missions, US Navy Hellcat VF 72

Ghisonaccia
310th BG, 324th FG, 350th FG

Migliacciaru

Ajaccio
350th FG,
Army Field Hospital

Solenzara
321st BG, 417th NFS (Beaufighter)

Bonifacio

N

0   10 miles

0   10km

ATTACKER'S CAPABILITIES

Air power against the Alps

The B-25s in Italy

B-25J "Ladies Delight" of the 486th Bomb Squadron with its escorts from the 57th Fighter Group. The bomber crews were always glad to see the fighter planes arrive to escort them over enemy-held territory, affectionately referring to them as "Our Little Brothers." (57th Bomb Wing Archives)

The North American B-25 Mitchell flown by the squadrons of the 57th Wing was considered by many to be the best American medium bomber of the war, and among the best medium bombers of any air force. The "definitive" sub-type was the B-25J, which entered production in late August 1943 at North America's Kansas City factory and became the most-produced version, with a production run of 4,390 out of a grand total of 9,890.

The first J-models arrived in the Mediterranean theater in March 1944, flown across the "Southern Route" from Florida over the Caribbean to Brazil thence across the South Atlantic to Africa and over the Sahara to Algeria. The first unit to completely re-equip was the 340th Bomb Group after its 88 B-25C and D models were destroyed by the volcanic ash from the eruption of Vesuvius that month, which covered the aircraft based at Pompeii airfield just to the southeast of the volcano, melting their plastic canopies and gun turrets and filling the fuselages with ash while burning the fabric off their control surfaces.

All three bomb groups of the 57th Wing had traded in the Mitchells they had flown in North Africa, Sicily, and Italy by mid-May following their move to Corsica. The 340th Group again lost over half their new bombers in the final Luftwaffe bombing raid in the MTO on the night of May 13/14; the surviving bombers would ever after be identifiable by the camouflage hurriedly painted on their upper surfaces afterwards. The event would be immortalized in *Catch 22*, written by a bombardier in the 340th's 488th Bomb Squadron, Joseph Heller, who arrived in the unit a week later.

The B-25 had a six-man crew: pilot, co-pilot, bombardier, flight engineer/top turret gunner, radioman/waist gunner, and tail gunner. The lead ship in a formation carried a seventh crewman, a navigator. The B-25Js of the 57th Wing could be distinguished from others by the removal of the four "package" .50cal machine guns, fitted two on each side externally on the forward fuselage sides below the cockpit, since these bombers were never

57th Bomb Wing Bombardment Groups and Squadrons

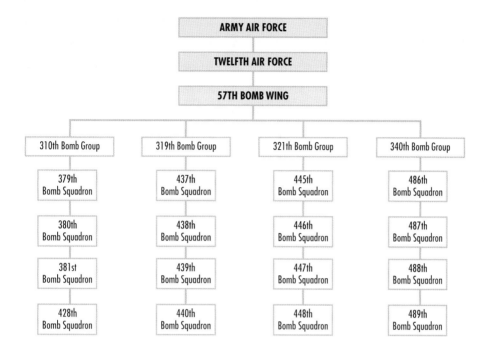

ABOVE 57TH BOMB WING ORGANIZATION

The battle for the Brenner Pass, the most successful battlefield interdiction campaign ever performed by the US Air Force, is given scant notice in wartime accounts of USAAF operations in the Mediterranean theater. As one wag put it, "The Air Force doesn't want to admit they ever did a good thing for the Army."

All night, hot ash fell on the 340th Bomb Group base at Pompeii when Vesuvius erupted in March 1944; although destruction was near total, there were no casualties. The entire fleet of bombers, about 88 B-25s, were lost. It is a tribute to American manufacturing that the 340th was back flying combat missions only one week later with replacement aircraft. (57th Bomb Wing Archives)

The young bombardier Joseph Heller, third from the left, top row, on Corsica. Other crewmen are unidentified. After the war, Heller wrote the novel *Catch-22*, drawing heavily on his experiences in the 488th Bomb Squadron. (57th Bomb Wing Archive, Burton Blume Collection)

employed in the strafing role. The B-25 could carry a maximum load of four 1,000lb bombs; these were always high-explosive (HE) bombs for the Brenner Pass campaign. An alternative load was eight 500lb HE bombs or ten sets of cluster incendiaries wired together so that the bundled bomblets separated when dropped, spreading the incendiaries over a wide area. Powered by two Wright R-2600 14 cylinder radial engines, the airplane had a top speed of 275mph and a cruising speed in formation of 230mph.

In October 1944, the Mediterranean Allied Tactical Air Forces (MATAF) – which comprised British and Commonwealth, Free French, and American units – were primarily located on Corsica. The force included two groups of USAAF medium bombers: the 42nd Bomb Wing, composed of three bomb groups flying B-26 Marauders, and the 57th Wing with three groups flying B-25 Mitchells. Additionally there were four USAAF fighter groups, all now flying the Republic P-47 Thunderbolt. The B-26 groups initiated attacks on the Po Valley and Brenner Pass rail lines in October as part of the attempt to cut off the German Tenth and Fourteenth armies from their supply bases in Germany. These attacks continued until November 21, 1944, when the 42nd Wing was transferred to France to reinforce the B-26 units of the 9th Air Force. This also rationalized the supply and spare parts system, since the B-26 was the only medium bomber operated by the USAAF in northwestern Europe, while the B-25 would now be the only US medium bomber operated in the MTO. This reduction in force continued in January 1945, when the 319th Bomb Group was detached from MATAF and returned to the United States to re-equip with the new Douglas A-26 Invader. The 12 squadrons of the 310th, 321st, and 340th groups of the 57th Wing were now the only medium bomber force left in the 12th Air Force, and were solely responsible for Operation *Bingo* between the end of December 1944 and the conclusion of the campaign on April 25, 1945. While the B-25s concentrated on rail bridges, stations, marshalling yards, and the rest of the infrastructure associated with the transport system, the P-47 fighter-bombers were tasked with attacking individual trains.

The fighter-bomber war

Four P-47-equipped groups in XXII Fighter Command participated in the battles over the Brenner Pass: the 57th, 79th, 324th, and 350th Fighter Groups. Originally based on Corsica, they would move to Grosseto on the Italian mainland shortly after the commencement of Operation *Bingo* in November 1944.

Longest-serving was the 57th Fighter Group, the first American fighter group to enter combat in Europe after they were transported in July 1942 to Accra, Ghana, aboard the carrier *Ranger*, then flew their P-40s on to Egypt where they operated with the RAF's Desert Air Force through the North African campaign and Sicily. Re-equipping with P-47s in December 1943, they were the group most closely involved in the Brenner battles.

The big P-47 was an even better fighter-bomber than it was a fighter, armed with eight .50cal machine guns and able to carry a 500lb bomb under each wing. They were frequently used to attack and suppress German antiaircraft positions, in addition to dive-bombing attacks against difficult bridge targets and roving hunts across northern Italy in search of trains and road traffic.

Among the 57th's pilots was Michael McCarthy, who arrived in the unit as a brand-new 2nd lieutenant a month before his 20th birthday, shortly after the Palm Sunday Massacre (an operation in which transport aircraft evacuating German forces from Tunisia suffered heavy losses) in April 1943, and became one of very few fighter-bomber pilots to survive two complete combat tours. He later wrote: "The air-to-ground environment is brutal, life threatening, and consistently dangerous. The fighter pilot population in our squadron changed 400 percent from May 1943 until the end of the war. We lost airplanes and pilots on a regular basis. We changed tactics, varied approaches and routes to targets, and emphasized surprise at every opportunity. In the end, we learned that you must fly down the enemy's gun barrel to destroy the target."

Alone among USAAF fighter units, the 57th Fighter Group followed a command philosophy that required proven ability in combat – not rank or time in the unit – be the basis for selection of element, section, flight, and squadron leaders. McCarthy recalled: "We followed that policy without exception during my 27 months with the group. In some cases, a captain or major, newly assigned, might fly a complete tour as a wingman and fail every chance to lead an element or a section. It was odd to see a squadron of 16 ships led successfully by a young first lieutenant with a field grade officer riding his wing, but the policy saved lives, put the strongest pilots in lead positions, and produced exceptional combat results." In the group, a new pilot was known as a "Sprog." Once he had survived 15–20 missions and demonstrated some ability, he was promoted to "Sport." If he survived half a tour, he became an "Old Sport." Those "Old Sports" who showed skill as well as ability were promoted into unit leadership as positions opened through completion of tour, transfer, or death, and were the "Wheels" of the group. McCarthy became one of those "Wheels" during his second tour, promoted to major and 65th Squadron Operations Officer a month before he turned 21.

The 57th Fighter Group arrived on Corsica in mid-March 1944, taking up residence at Alto airfield, near the town of

Corsica was made up of agricultural and fishing villages, with very little in the way of nightlife, so the GIs had to make their own entertainment. Here we see a comedy skit in progress. Note the orchestra: it was made up of men from the 321st Bomb Group who called themselves "The Mitchell Aires." (57th Bomb Wing Archives)

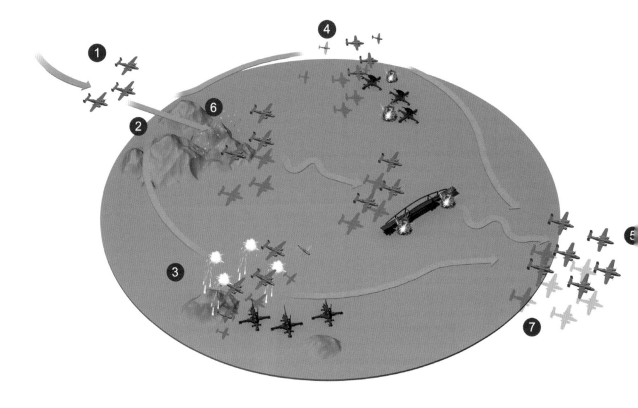

ABOVE BOMBING RUN

1. The bombing run begins with the advanced flight of three or, in this case, six lead ships of the anti-flak formation. They come in about six miles ahead of the main formation, at a lower altitude (9,000ft) than the main formation (11,000ft), and at a different speed. This is to force the computer controlling the guns to constantly need to recalculate.

2. As they crest the mountain and become visible to the German ranging radar, the formation drops chaff, also known as "Window" – small, thin strips of aluminum which are almost weightless, and will linger in the air for a long time. The cloud of chaff reflects the radar beams and obscures the location of the incoming aircraft formations.

3. The right echelon peels off to attack a gun battery in the hills. They drop white phosphorus, which produces obscuring white smoke and horrific burns to anyone it lands on, causing the gun crews to seek shelter until the danger passes.

4. The left echelon peels off to attack another battery with fragmentation bombs. The anti-flak formation is escorted by three P-47 fighters which fly above the B-25s on the bomb run, but which would sometimes also strafe the gun batteries.

5. The two echelons re-form the six-plane box as they exit the valley over the mountains, and the fighters resume their escort position above the bombers.

6. With the German guns hopefully silenced, the bomber formation (12 to 18 aircraft) crest the mountains. From the Initial Point (IP) just on the other side of the mountain to "Bombs Away" they must fly straight and steady. If the guns are intact they are sitting ducks for the German gun crews who scramble back to their posts as soon as the danger from the anti-flak echelons has passed. Very often the ships in the last formation would find themselves under heavy fire.

7. After "Bombs Away!" the aircraft are now free to take evasive action. As a group they dive from 11,000ft to descend at least 500–1,000ft and make a 20-degree turn. After making the initial turn, the German targeting computers will plot their anticipated location and fire a volley. It will take around ten seconds for the 88mm rounds to reach an altitude of 10,000ft, so the pilots must change direction every ten seconds to stay ahead of the computer's calculations and the flight time of the rounds. With the 3,000–4,000lb bomb load gone, the powerful engines are able to gain altitude without losing much speed. They regain their altitude as they crest the mountain and get out of range of the guns.

Folleli, north of what would become the three B-25 fields. Advance parties had arrived early enough to set up tents and prepare mess halls, clubs, and maintenance facilities. Since they had been doing this for almost two years, they knew all the short-cuts and problem areas. In fact, the 57th had a well-deserved reputation as the best scroungers in the Mediterranean theater. If they needed something and could not borrow or buy it, they had a team of "midnight requisitioners" who would steal it. "Our road convoys were so diverse that it was difficult to identify the national identity of most of our vehicles. We had more German, Italian, and British rolling stock than American." McCarthy recounted. After the North African desert and the dusty heat of Sicily, Corsica was a big change. McCarthy remembered: "After a tediously long hot day on the line, ground crews and pilots relaxed in the cool invigorating mountain stream. Improvised diving boards were constructed. Life in the mountains afforded a great many men a chance to rest in quiet and take things easy for a while but for others who craved excitement, the complaint was that life was growing monotonous and dull."

"The Jug," as the P-47 was universally known to its pilots throughout the war, was a great dive-bomber because it had excellent stability at all speeds. McCarthy wrote: "It was easy to center the ball, trim, and keep the nose on the target. It was a relief not to stand on the left rudder just to keep the airplane from slipping sideways in a dive (as was the case with the P-40). This natural stability enhanced an excellent gun platform. Strafing a fast-moving train in the Po Valley later in the war, I hit the locomotive with the cone of my eight guns knocking it completely off the tracks while the rest of the train, minus its locomotive, rolled on with no hesitation."

During their time in Corsica, the pilots would discover just how hard their mission was. McCarthy remembered one song that was frequently sung after a few drinks in the Officer's Club:

THE DIVE BOMBER'S LAMENT
I don't mind a dive in a 25
Till the bombs that I'm carrying smack
But those little black flowers
That grow in the sky –
Oh! My achin' back.
Skimmin' a ridge to plaster a bridge
Makes you feel as goofy as wine,
And your heart takes a jolt
when your Thunderbolt
Tangles with an Me-109.

It's like shootin' ducks
When you come across trucks
And I don't mind the rifles that crack.
But those little black flowers
That grow in the sky –
Oh! My achin' back!

A view of the Brenner Pass, the principal route for supplying the German armies in Italy. The meandering Adige River and its tributaries required multiple bridges throughout the rail line. (57th Bomb Wing Archives)

That so many pilots survived in this brutal environment was due to the toughness of the P-47. McCarthy described the airplane: "It could absorb heavy flak damage and still fly. The big Pratt and Whitney engine was incredibly tough. I flew one from Italy to Corsica taking 45 minutes with zero oil pressure minus two top cylinders that had been blown off by enemy fire. The engine ran until I pulled the throttle back for landing. That was not a fluke. Another squadron pilot repeated this later without three top cylinders and zero oil pressure. The secret was not to change the power setting."

After one air battle in May 1944, McCarthy heard a call for help from a fellow 65th Squadron pilot: "I found him circling with his wingman in the area just vacated by those involved in the dogfight. One 20-mm shell had knocked out his instrument panel, leaving him without airspeed, altimeter, compass, or engine performance gauges. The second shell hit his right wing ammo compartment, exploding many .50-caliber bullets and forcing the door from its normal horizontal position to a vertical position that disturbed the aerodynamic flow across the wing, making the airplane fly in a severe crab. This was another example of a P-47 defying the principles of flight, flyable despite serious airframe damage." After examining the airplane from every angle, McCarthy determined it wasn't leaking fluids and had no obvious structural damage other than that to the right wing and the cockpit area. "We decided I would lead back to Corsica with him on my wing. Because of the deformed right wing ammo compartment, we needed to identify the airspeed at which the airplane would stall so we could pick a final approach airspeed for landing. At Alto, we circled the field high enough to permit a safe bailout. In the landing configuration, I slowed from 220mph calling the airspeed in 5mph increments. He found the pre-stall shudder began just below 170mph so we chose that speed for our final approach. I held 185mph as we turned to line up on final, slowing very smoothly to 170mph as we crossed the fence. He held excellent position, rotated, and touched down nicely with plenty of room to slow to taxi speed on the available runway." The P-47 had brought another pilot home safe in conditions no other airplane could have survived.

Every moment of a fighter-bomber mission was filled with potential danger that could become reality in an instant. On one mission, McCarthy led his flight in a successful

From left to right: General Ira Eaker, Commander of the Mediterranean Allied Air Forces; General Robert Knapp, Commander of 57th Bomb Wing; General John Cannon, Commander of 12 Air Force; Colonel Peter Remington, Commanding Officer of the 310th Bomb Group. (57th Bomb Wing Archives)

dive-bombing attack against marshalling yards. Since they still had ammunition after dropping their bombs, he led the others on a low-level "armed recce" hunting mission until he found a train in the open on a straight stretch of track. Deploying two elements to cut the track ahead of and behind the train, McCarthy then attacked the steam locomotive, which brought the train to a halt. "I set up my section to strafe freight cars immediately behind the disabled locomotive. I told my wingman to take enough space, keep me in sight, pick his own freight car, and do some damage. We were taking some light

The aftermath of the Luftwaffe attack on Alesani airfield in May 1944. The attack came at night, when the bombers were fueled and loaded with bombs ready for the morning mission. The 340th Bomb Group lost nearly all of its aircraft to the German air raid. (© Hymie Setzer Collection)

flak, less intense than usual. My wingman stayed much too close to me on the first strafing pass, so close that his bullets flew over the top of my right wing, shooting at the same freight car." McCarthy ordered the young lieutenant to move out further so he could concentrate on his own target and get some worthwhile results.

While the wingman's spacing was better on the next pass, he had managed to line up on the only obstacle within miles – a lone pine tree 100ft tall. "Lieutenant Brown, who never saw that tree, hit it dead center with the hub of his four-bladed propeller, which sawed through the pine tree, and filled the engine space full of wood chips and sawdust." The impact of the collision also knocked both wings back, out of alignment. Through a combination of luck and the remarkable resilience of the tough P-47, Brown stayed airborne. "Understandably, he was in total panic. I caught sight of his airplane in a slight climb heading north, and pulled up on his wing."

McCarthy surveyed the damage, amazed any airplane could fly in that condition. Talking calmly on the radio, he told Brown to look at him, that they would keep on climbing, and he should not touch his throttle. After a few minutes, McCarthy told Brown they were going to turn left back to Corsica. "If the controls responded well enough and the engine continued to run without drastic overheating, I planned to climb high enough to allow a safe bail out over water in case the engine quit. We had alerted the air rescue guys about that possibility." The P-47's windshield had been crazed in the collision and covered with oil and debris. "I told him that I would navigate back to base. As minutes passed with the damaged airplane still flying, it was likely we would get home, but that raised a question. How do we get this wreck safely on the ground?"

Once they arrived back over Alto at 6,000ft, McCarthy told his wingman to drop the landing gear. The main gear fell out of the gear wells without hydraulic pressure and seemed to lock down. McCarthy sat on Brown's wing as the two P-47s executed a circling descent to turn on their final approach. Fortunately, Brown was able to retard his throttle without killing the engine. McCarthy moved forward so Brown could fly formation on him due to the fact he couldn't see the runway through his windshield. Brown managed to touch down successfully, at which point McCarthy accelerated and came around for his own landing. He later remembered: "Lieutenant Brown handled himself with courage and skill but decided his luck was gone. He did not fly another mission and neither did that airplane."

During the fall of 1944, the Thunderbolt became an even more formidable weapon than before with the arrival of "bazooka" rocket tubes. Each P-47 could carry six rocket tubes, three under each wing hanging from the underwing pylon, which could be jettisoned in

Time-lapse photo of a P-47
firing a rocket. (57th
Bomb Wing Archives,
Burton Blume Collection)

Time-lapse photo of a P-47 firing a rocket. (57th Bomb Wing Archives, Burton Blume Collection)

an emergency. The rockets were initially popular, since they took a heavy toll of enemy installations and supplies. However, a problem was quickly discovered: the tubes the rockets were fired from were made of plastic, which inevitably deformed after only a few firings. McCarthy recalled that pilots soon discovered that by the second or third mission where rockets were employed, out of the six rockets fired, at least one could be expected to come out of the tube and execute "a looping roll" that could scare the pilot with a near miss. The rockets were not particularly accurate, but were good enough to make flak gunners take cover as the P-47s made their dive-bombing attacks. P-47s began coming off the production lines in November 1944 with factory-fitted underwing pylons, instead of the field-fitted pylons that had become available over the summer and fall. These factory-installed pylons were capable of carrying a 1,000lb bomb, which greatly increased the capability of the airplane as a dive bomber.

First Lieutenant James L. Diers joined the 64th Fighter Squadron in the fall of 1944, after the 57th Fighter Group had moved to the coastal town of Grosseto on the Italian mainland to put them closer to the fighting, where they would remain to the end of the war. By now, the main enemy was the German and Italian antiaircraft gunners, who had become very good at their work.

Forty years later, Diers was asked what it was like to make a dive-bombing attack on the German antiaircraft positions. He recalled: "Once we were over our target and began our dive to release our bombs, all evasive action ceased. We just dove down as fast as possible from about 4,000 feet to a few hundred, pulled the release lever, and dropped the bombs on our target. During those few seconds I felt no sense of danger, no fear of the guns, just concentration on my dive. Bravery was not a factor. Being young and feeling immortal was. But, post dive, I'll admit to a bit of anxiety as I climbed upward out of range of all those black puffs in the sky around me and out of the area as fast as possible, full throttle!"

Since it had been the first American fighter unit to enter combat in the Mediterranean, the 57th Fighter Group set records the other groups couldn't match. In December 1944, the three squadrons became the first and only USAAF fighter squadrons of the war to each fly 1,000 missions. The 66th Squadron hit that mark on December 13, the 64th on December 22, and the 65th on Christmas Eve. The 57th Group was credited with its 3,000th mission on December 31, with the 66th Squadron getting the honor of flying the mission. The record grew to 4,000 missions at the end of February 1945. By the end of the war in Italy, the group had flown a total of 4,651 missions since August 1942, including 35 missions over May 1 and 2, 1945, the final days of the Italian campaign.

The morale problem in the 57th Bomb Wing

Perhaps the biggest problem the campaign faced was the morale of the aircrews. After Italy was declared a "secondary theater" after the Normandy invasion in June 1944, getting replacements became difficult. From their arrival in North Africa in 1943, the standard tour for B-25 aircrews had been 50 missions. Following the departure of the 42nd Bomb Wing and later the 319th Bomb Group, not only was the 57th Bomb Wing left alone on Corsica, but the overall downgrading of the MTO as compared with the European and Pacific theaters meant that so few replacements arrived that the mission tour in the wing was raised from 60 in October to 65 in November, and finally 70 in December. At one point in November, the 340th group had 45 crews qualified to go home with 60 missions; however, doing so would leave only 22 crews, with no replacements on the horizon. While many men grumbled about this and the war diarist for the 340th Bomb Group wrote about "a severe loss of morale" among the fliers of the group, men gradually became resigned to their fate. Paul Young, who had been made a first pilot in early December, told the 445th Squadron's operations officer that he was willing to fly any pilot assignment – first pilot or co-pilot – that came up. "It was the only way I could think of to get all the way to 70 missions and go home."

As winter weather further reduced the days on which missions could be flown, the strain on the men of trying to get enough missions to go home grew worse. There were no regularly assigned crews, as was the case in the Eighth and Fifteenth strategic air forces, and it was thus

not uncommon for the six men in a bomber to be complete strangers. On one occasion, a crew that ended up in Switzerland after their plane was badly shot up over the target was asked to identify the pilot, who had been killed in the crash. The radioman recalled: "None of us knew who he was; we'd never flown with him till that mission."

Bombing accuracy

General Knapp graded his group commanders on their unit's bombing accuracy as revealed in post-strike photos. Thus, the group commanders stressed bombing accuracy to their squadron commanders, who in turn ordered the crews to fly straight and level bomb runs of at least four minutes from the "initial point" to "bombs away." Crews were reluctant to do so because this was enough time for the German gunners to fire several volleys, and was the point in any mission when most flak hits and shooting-downs happened.

The 445th Bomb Squadron developed a tactic to minimize their exposure. Foremost among the leading squadron members was Dan Bowling, who arrived on Corsica in late August after traveling across the Atlantic on a Victory ship converted to a hospital ship that took 21 days to get from Norfolk, Virginia, to Naples in Italy. Three weeks after he arrived at the 321st's base at Solenzara airfield, Bowling turned 22. Raised in the hardscrabble mining town of Bisbee, Arizona, which he remembered as "a company town through and through," Bowling had learned early in life to never back down from a fight; his father was a union organizer and the children of the miners at the Phelps-Dodge Corporation who had turned against his family picked on him at school. He thus arrived on Corsica with a reputation for not "taking guff" from anyone he had come across in the Army, regardless of rank, when he believed those in authority were wrong.

During training, the Air Force recognized Bowling's leadership qualities when he was made cadet company

Captain Dan Bowling, a pilot of the 321st Bombardment Group, 445th Bomb Squadron. His fellow pilot, Paul Young, said of Bowling: "He was the squadron leader – that's different from the squadron commander." (57th Bomb Wing Archives)

commander of each of the units he passed through on the way to pinning on his pilot's wings. Following graduation from flight school, he was fortunate to have been the beneficiary of additional training before being posted overseas, which meant he held a "green card" as a fully trained pilot capable of instrument flying. This made him unique among all the pilots in the group other than the Group Commander. On his third training flight, Bowling was told by the pilot checking him out that he had more hours as a B-25 first pilot than did his training officer. Within a matter of days after being signed off, he had flown his first combat mission as a first pilot, and after four missions in his first week, he was put into training to become a "lead pilot." By the end of September, Bowling was a flight leader, responsible for two wingmen. Bowling soon connected with bombardier 1st Lieutenant Joe Silnutzer. By late October, they were considered by their squadron mates to be the best pilot-bombardier crew in the unit. Paul Jackson remembered Bowling thus: "He was the squadron leader – that's different from the squadron commander."

Bowling and Silnutzer decided to find a way to avoid or at least minimize exposure to the enemy and still hit the target with an accurate drop. Bowling recalled: "Joe and I decided that the only way to survive our missions was by performing evasive action. We practiced many times on the bomb range. We would fly a certain compass heading to the practice target circle, then turn ten to fifteen degrees right or left, then change again to a different compass heading and immediately change to the exact course to target. Joe's timing with that Norden sight was so accurate that we would only need to spend thirty to forty seconds straight and level to the target." What Silnutzer learned to do was feed in these evasive maneuvers to the computer in the bomb sight. While they were working out their evasion tactic, Bowling was made a squadron lead pilot and Silnutzer a squadron lead bombardier. Bowling recalled what then happened: "When I was out front ahead of everyone else, they had to do what I did, so they followed me. I could look out just after we changed course and see a barrage of flak go off right where we would have been had we continued on. Then we'd turn and there would be another barrage go off where we would have been. When we turned on to the bomb run, the gunners were so confused they didn't have the time to put up that last volley before we dropped and broke formation."

Only a few other lead crew pilot-bombardier teams tried to emulate Bowling's evasive tactic. Colonel Smith, the 321st's group commander, was quite open that "I want a star when I leave" and ordered the group to make straight-and-level six-minute bomb runs so he could impress General Knapp with the strike photos. Writing of his wartime experiences, Bowling recalled: "After the Colonel had repeated his order during a pre-mission briefing and had left the room, I told the other pilots to follow me. I was proud of two things about the missions I led. One was that we had the highest bombing accuracy of anybody in the group; we never missed a target. And the other was that I had the lowest losses of any missions. We got the target and we didn't lose our friends."

Eventually, 445th Squadron commander Lt Colonel Cassidy ceased arguing with Bowling about his tactic. Instead, Bowling received the highest unspoken praise possible: he was the pilot picked to lead the squadron on every tough mission during the worst period of the battles over the Brenner toward the end of the war. This was all despite the fact that Army Intelligence considered him a potential "security risk" due to his father's "subversive politics," which resulted in an Army Intelligence officer, playing the role of a squadron ground officer, being assigned to watch Bowling throughout the war.

Pilot Dan Bowling on the right with his bombardier, Joe Silnutzer. These two men worked together to figure out an evasive action procedure which would successfully avoid being targeted by flak and still put them on the target. After they proved the technique, they trained other crews in its use. (57th Bomb Wing Archives)

OPPOSITE SHORAN OPERATION

SHORAN: the system that defeated the weather

The major impediment to the campaign was the winter weather. The record shows that between November 6, 1944, and April 25, 1945, there were 116 completely clear days over the Brenner Pass and another 40 where the bombers were still able to carry out missions despite the poor weather. What was needed was something that made the weather problem if not irrelevant, then at least not so important. The "something" that solved the problem was SHORAN (SHOrt Range Aerial Navigation), which first arrived in the 310th Group in December 1944. Once the group's lead navigators and bombardiers were trained in its use, they taught their skills to the 321st and 340th groups during February and the first missions were flown against Brenner targets in March.

The SHORAN system used two radio transmitting stations, one high frequency and one low frequency. The equipment in the aircraft being guided by the system included a transmitter, a receiver, an operator's console, and a K-1A bombing computer. The transmitter sent radio pulses to one of the ground stations, then to the other. The bombing computer calculated the distance in miles to the particular station by clocking the elapsed time between the transmitter pulse and the returned signal. As the aircraft flew toward the target, the low-frequency station was on the left, and the high-frequency station on the right, which allowed the computer to triangulate the two stations and the target, whose location was known. Unlike the similar British "Oboe" blind bombing system, SHORAN could guide multiple aircraft simultaneously, whereas "Oboe" could only guide one airplane at a time. The lead bombers were equipped with the equipment, and the lead bombardier dropped when the computer placed the airplane over the target, with the others in the formation dropping on his lead. This allowed the bombers to go after fixed targets such as marshalling yards or loading stations regardless of the weather.

The major limitation of SHORAN was that the system was limited to line-of-sight ultra-high frequency (UHF) radio communication, which required the transmitting airplane to fly at altitudes above 14,000ft, depending on local geography, which was a difficult feat in a loaded B-25 without an oxygen system.

With SHORAN, the mission rate nearly doubled, the only limiting factor being cloud cover that extended above 15,000ft, the maximum altitude at which the Mitchells could fly. Sergeant Jerry Rosenthal of the 488th Squadron recalled that by early March, he had 30 missions; by the end of April, after the squadron started using SHORAN, his mission total was 70.

Fighting the cold

In addition to the scarcity of good bombardment targets, other factors made interdiction particularly difficult. The rugged mountainous terrain of Italy imposed burdens on aircraft and the combat crews by forcing them to fly at 13,000, 14,000, and even 15,000ft to reach their objectives. The B-25s had only limited heating, and the oxygen systems had been removed due to fire danger from flak hits. Jerry Rosenthal remembered: "Anoxia [oxygen deficiency] was a big problem, since the missions into the Brenner Pass were generally flown at 11,500 to 15,000ft. We would take our gloves off to check our fingernails for signs of anoxia even though we couldn't do anything about it. We also got to know all about *aerotitis media*, the inflammation of the inner ear from changes in altitude. The air temperature in the airplane at my station as radioman was around 25 below, and if you took off your

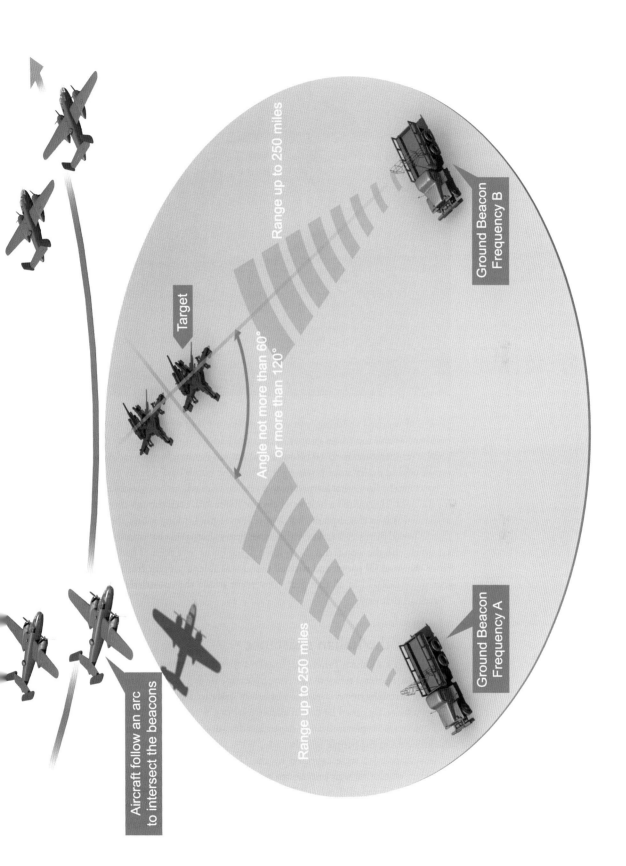

Aircraft follow an arc to intersect the beacons

Range up to 250 miles

Target

Angle not more than 60° or more than 120°

Range up to 250 miles

Ground Beacon Frequency A

Ground Beacon Frequency B

The B-25s had no on-board heating system, and winter temperatures over the Alps could be 40 degrees below zero. Gunners were warned not to touch the .50cal guns with their bare hands, or their fingers would stick to the metal. (57th Bomb Wing Archives)

glove and touched anything, you could freeze your skin to whatever it was. The pilots and bombardier and top turret gunner in the nose had a couple [of] heaters there that probably got the temperature up to 10 below, as did the tail gunner. But the radioman's position was unheated and drafty since it was right behind the bomb bay."

Fortunately, Rosenthal learned from a veteran with whom he shared a tent how to prepare for the cold. "I acquired a blue wool electric flight suit, even though there was no electricity available for it in the airplane, but I wore it over my GI long johns, then a wool shirt over that followed by my A-2 jacket with a super heavy sheepskin coat over that! Wool socks, then GI shoes with the wonderful sheep-lined flying boots over them. I had sheepskin overalls to cover the wool GI pants, and with all that, I was able to prevent frostbite!" He also recalled that when encased in all that gear, movement inside the constricted space of the fuselage "wasn't all that easy."

An ally: the Italian resistance

It took only a moment for chance to take a flier from the fear of trying to survive a tough mission to the abject terror of surviving his escape from a shot-up, burning bomber. After the shock of throwing oneself into the vastness of space to depend on a parachute, knowing that many failed, a flier then landed in enemy territory, where he was hunted by German troops and Italian fascist paramilitaries, dependent for survival – if not immediately captured – on the kindness of the people of Italy.

Americans who were captured by the Germans were generally transported north to Germany, where they were imprisoned in POW camps, though by 1945 – when transportation to Germany became difficult – POW camps were organized in northern Italy. Those captured by the RSI (*Repubblica Sociale Italiana*, the puppet Italian Social Republic set up by the Germans) paramilitaries had a higher likelihood of being shot than if they were taken by the Germans; if they made it into captivity, they were then turned over to the Germans.

Escape and evasion for downed airmen was easier in Italy than in Germany, since they were held only a hundred miles or so beyond the front lines, which meant they had a good chance of getting back to Allied territory if they were picked up by partisans. While Mussolini's fascists had controlled Italy since 1922, they had not succeeded in completely repressing their leftist opposition, which had gone underground in the years before the war. With the arrival of the Allies in 1943 and the subsequent Italian surrender and change of sides, the anti-fascist opposition groups resurfaced. In the fall of 1943, the *Comitato di Liberazione Nazionale* (Committee of National Liberation, or CLN) was formed by the *Partito Communista Italiana* (the Communist Party), the *Partito Socialista* (the Socialist Party), and the *Partito d'Azione* (a republican liberal party). The *Democrazia Cristiana* (Christian Democrats) took bureaucratic control of the movement as its public leaders, in alliance with King Victor Emmanuel III's government and the Allies. The CLN organized resistance in German-controlled northern Italy, and had the support of most anti-fascist groups in the region, which were usually from the Communists, the Socialists, or the *Partito d'Azione.* The armed partisan guerrilla groups included the communist Garibaldi Brigades, the *Giustizia e Libertà* (Justice and Freedom) Brigades of the *Partito d'Azione*, and the socialist Matteotti Brigades.

A partisan unit was usually composed of 20–50 members, the number governed by the group's ability to arm, clothe, and feed them and the degree of local support. The largest groups operated in the Alps and the Appenine mountains, where they ambushed and harassed the Germans and their RSI Italian puppets, who attempted to separate the guerrillas from their peasant supporters with a policy of killing ten Italians for any German or RSI man killed; the result was an increase in support for the partisans, who came from the peasant communities.

Even with the efforts of the Resistance, most Italians in the region controlled by the Germans did not want to become involved with any downed Allied flyers. This was because

A German flak battery in a redoubt. The built-up walls of the redoubts provided very good protection for the guns and crews, requiring a direct hit to take them out. (ullstein bild/Getty Images)

the Wehrmacht and the Italian fascist paramilitary groups had a policy of immediate execution for any Italian found helping Allied airmen, a punishment that could be extended to an entire family if they were thought to have participated in hiding the captured Allied flyer. The common people were caught in the middle, along with the young Americans on the run.

Over 100 members of the 57th Bomb Wing were rescued by the Italian partisans during the Brenner campaign. Most were smuggled through the lines and returned to the Allies, but several were hidden by families until the end of the war in villages where everyone knew the Americans were among them, yet no one ever turned them in to the enemy.

The story of the 445th Squadron crew led by pilot 2nd Lieutenant Jay DeBoer is representative of the differing fates experienced by aircrew forced to bail out. Their bomber, "Miss Bobby," was assigned to flak suppression on February 27, 1945. Neither DeBoer, bombardier Flight Officer William Brooks, co-pilot 2nd Lieutenant Lucian Crutchfield, navigator 2nd Lieutenant Robert "Bob" Cravey, nor Sergeants Robert Mitchell, Charles Reagin, or Carl Swinson saw any gunfire until an 88mm shell exploded in the right engine, which burst into flames that quickly spread. DeBoer fought to fly the barely controllable B-25 westward to get as far as possible from the Germans they had just showered with deadly white phosphorus. Nevertheless, within minutes, the flames forced the men to bail out over the village of Vezzano in the Italian Tyrol.

On the snow-covered wooded hillside below, 22-year-old Giovanni Cainelli, 36-year-old Vigilio Paissan, and six others watched the crew bail out. "It seemed like they took a long time to come down and that gave us enough time to get to where they landed at about the same time they did," Cainelli recalled. "We had to hurry because the Germans were coming up the mountain with dogs. We knew that the partisans were also headed our way." Navigator Bob Cravey and tail gunner Carl Swinson were lucky to be found by

Headquarters of the 340th Bombardment Group on Corsica. The 340th operated from the base at Alesani from April 1944 until March 1945. (57th Bomb Wing Archives)

Cainelli. The baying dogs leading the Germans up the hillside could be heard approaching as partisans led by 40-year-old Roberto "Berto" Peterlanna appeared out of the woods. Cravey asked hopefully: "Do any of you speak English?"

Peterlanna laughed. "Sure," he replied, "I spent fifteen years in New Jersey." He ordered Cainelli and the others to go before the Germans found them, and led the two Americans into the woods. Taking them to a nearby farm, he told them to hide in the barn.

Co-pilot Lucian Crutchfield broke his ankle getting out of the plane and landed further down the mountainside from where Cravey and Swinson had been rescued by the partisans. As he looked for something to splint his ankle, he was knocked over by a dog that pinned him down. He stared up at the black uniform of a Waffen-SS trooper, who pointed a sub-machine gun at him; all he could do was raise his hands. Not far away, bombardier Bill Brooks landed in a tree, his parachute caught in its branches. As he tried to cut himself free, he heard the dogs and looked down at two German Shepherds.

A moment later, two Waffen-SS troopers appeared. He too raised his hands in surrender.

The sun had already gone behind the tall Alpine hills when the SS men and their two American captives appeared in Vezzano. They went to the police station and put their prisoners in a cell for the night.

Jay DeBoer, who landed alone in the middle of the forest, where he fell into a large snowbank, spent the frigid night curled in an empty animal den he found.

The next morning, the Germans marched Brooks and Crutchfield out of the village. With Brooks helping, Crutchfield managed to stumble downhill for about a kilometer before he tripped and fell, crying out in agony. As Brooks turned to help, one of the SS troopers yelled at him. There was a burst of machine-gun fire and both Americans fell into the roadside ditch. DeBoer, hiding in the nearby woods, saw the Germans check them and then leave. He retreated further into the woods.

After several days, DeBoer was so hungry he no longer cared if he was captured. Coming across a peasant's hut, he decided to knock and accept whatever happened. As luck had it, the hut was a partisan base. He spent a week regaining strength before they took him to the rail station. Disguised as a Trappist monk, which explained his refusal to talk, he traveled the route his comrades were bombing. He made it into Switzerland in late March and returned to the 445th Squadron at their new base in Italy after the war ended.

Berto's partisan group took Cravey and Swinson to Cadine, a village of 300 some 3km from Vezzano. Partisans Vigilio, Mario, and Angelo Paissan hid them in the home of the family matriarch, where Angelo, his wife, and two children, and Mario with his wife and four daughters also lived. Years later, Vigilio recalled: "The whole town knew where the Americans were, but nobody talked. They were lucky they met good people because everybody knew the penalty for harboring Americans was death. They were hidden in a secret, tiny room in the basement of my brothers' house." Cravey and Swinson remained in Cadine until they were liberated by troops of the 10th Mountain Division at the end of April 1945.

Radioman Tech Sergeant Charles T. Reagin and turret gunner Sergeant Robert D. Mitchell were captured by the Germans only moments after they landed and were taken to a POW camp, where they remained until liberated in May 1945.

The antiflak element has dropped white phosphorus on AA gun positions in the Brenner Pass. The US Army declared the purpose was to obscure the gunners' sighting of the incoming bomber formation, but when the phosphorus drifted onto gun positions, it would cause severe burns on exposed skin. The Germans insisted that it was chemical warfare, in violation of the Geneva Convention. (57th Bomb Wing Archives)

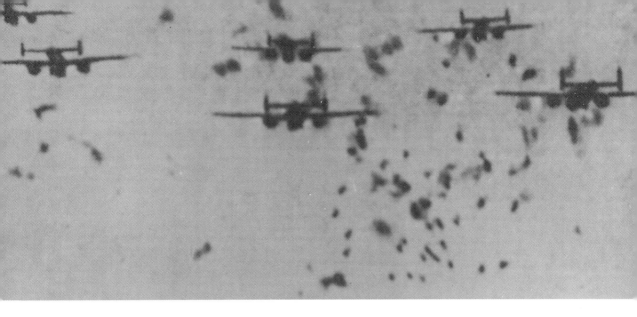

DEFENDER'S CAPABILITIES
Flak, smoke, and fighters

Air defense

Ships of the 487th Bomb Squadron brave a flak barrage. Depending upon circumstances, flak guns could use fire-control targeting or simply throw up a barrage into a single concentrated point in the sky. Flying into a barrage was terrifying to the crews, but their odds of being shot down were actually far less than when being individually targeted. (57th Bomb Wing Archives)

The *Repubblica Sociale Italiana* was formed after the rescue of Mussolini by SS commando Otto Skorzeny on September 24, 1943, from the Gran Sasso, where his Italian captors had imprisoned him. The state declared Rome its capital but was *de facto* based in Salò (thus its colloquial name, *Repubblica di Salò,* Republic of Salò), a small town on Lake Garda, near Brescia, where Mussolini and the Ministry of Foreign Affairs were headquartered.

The division of the *Regia Aeronautica* (Italian Royal Air Force) following Mussolini's dismissal and imprisonment in July 1943 fell largely along geographical lines, with units in the Allied-controlled area largely going over to the Allies to form the Italian Co-Belligerent Air Force, but those in the German-controlled region remaining loyal to the fascist government in the National Republican Air Force (*Aeronautica Nazionale Repubblicana,* or ANR). ANR combat operations began in December 1943, with the squadrons operating Macchi C.205 Veltro and Fiat G.55 Centauro fighters. In January 1944, the C.205s of the 1st Squadriglia "Asso di Bastoni" engaged in combat with a formation of P-38 Lightnings, three of which were shot down. In April 1944, the German military authorities ordered the incorporation of the ANR into the Luftwaffe, but the Italian pilots burned their fighters in protest. Beginning in June 1944, the ANR was re-equipped with Messerschmitt Bf 109G-6 and later G-10 and G-14 fighters.

The last Luftwaffe fighter unit departed Italy following the fall of Rome, leaving the ANR pilots with responsibility for the air defense of northern Italy. Between October 1944 and February 1945, 2° Gruppo Caccia "Gigi Tre Osei" was the only ANR fighter unit active in the defense of northern Italy. From November 1944, casualties began to outnumber victories for the Italian pilots. The 1° Gruppo Caccia "Asso di Bastoni" returned to Italy in February 1945, but the losses suffered by 2° Gruppo Caccia that fall meant that throughout the Brenner campaign, both ANR fighter groups never had more than 50 fighters available at any given time. Throughout the Brenner Pass bombing campaign, there were long periods without sufficient fuel available to make an effective defensive effort, since the Romanian

The Kommandogerät 40. This optical rangefinding device required 11 skilled men to operate. Settings were transmitted to an analog computer and the results sent to the gunners to sight the 88mm antiaircraft guns. (AKG-images)

oil fields around Ploesti had largely been destroyed by the XV Air Force during the spring and summer of 1944, followed by the success of the VIII Air Force campaign against the German synthetic oil industry. By September 1944, all German forces and their allies on all fronts were constantly short of fuel.

Six ANR pilots scored five or more victories against the Allies, including *Maggiore* (Major) Mario Bellagambi, commander of the 5th Squadriglia "Diavolo Rossi" of the 2° Gruppo Caccia, who scored ten of his total of 14 World War II victories with the ANR and was the second-highest-scoring ANR pilot.

Smoke generation

The Germans generated smoke using chlorosulphonic acid, which created smoke when exposed to the air. An effective density could be generated in approximately 20 minutes, so the defenders only activated the smoke generators some 30–35 minutes before an attack. Smoke generation was not reliable due to wind patterns in the Brenner Pass, which could blow away even a thick cover. January and February saw the most extensive use of smoke generation, which was most effective in the Lavis–San Michele region of the Adige River valley, due to the narrowness of the pass at this point. When used, the smokescreens created difficulty for both the defensive gunners, who might be unable to visually aim their weapons, and for the aircraft if the target was blanketed. Use of smoke was only reported on 18 missions, just five of which saw the smoke effective enough to interfere with accurate bombing. The most successful use of smoke occurred on January 22 at San Michele, when only three of 17 bombers were able to bomb their targets.

Antiaircraft artillery

The primary and most effective defense was provided by antiaircraft artillery. The Germans realized the mortal threat an air campaign against the Brenner railroad represented. Thus, the IV Flak Korps manned 366 88mm antiaircraft guns stationed between Verona and Innsbruck on November 1, 1944. This number would grow to nearly 500 guns by March 1945. The guns were crewed by the 5th and 137th Flak Regiments.

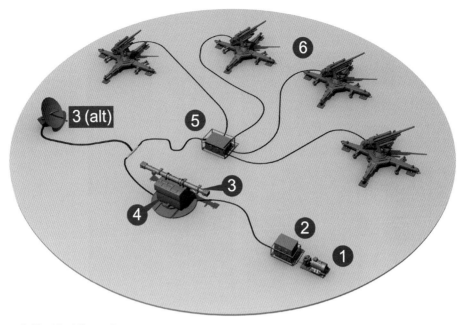

1. Electrical Generator
2. Control Box
3. Stereoscopic Range Finder
3 (alt). Some batteries substituted a radar for the stereoscopic range finder. However, it was considered to be less accurate than the manual range finder.
4. Mechanical Analog Command Computer
5. Signal Distribution Box
6. Gun Batterie

ABOVE FLAK BATTERY

The Germans and their Italian allies used a variety of weapons to defend the Brenner Pass railway. The primary antiaircraft artillery used by the Germans to defend the Brenner Pass rail line was officially known as the 8.8cm Flak 18, introduced into service in 1928 and designed by Krupp. Further development in the late 1930s resulted in the improved 8.8cm Flak 36, which had a two-piece barrel for easier replacement of worn liners, and later the 8.8cm Flak 37, which included updated instrumentation to allow the gun layers to follow directions from the single director more easily. "Flak" is a contraction of "*Flugabwehrkanone*" (also referred to as "*Fliegerabwehrkanone*"), which translates as "aircraft-defense cannon." In English, "flak" became a generic term for ground antiaircraft fire; the "88" was widely used by Germany throughout World War II, also in an antitank role, and is one of the most recognized German weapons of the conflict. Informally, the guns were universally known as the *Acht-acht* ("eight-eight") by the Germans and simply called the "88" by the Allies. The 88 could fire a 9.24kg (20.34lb) shell to over 49,000ft, far above the operating altitude of the 57th Wing's B-25s. The high muzzle velocity, combined with a heavy projectile, made the 8.8cm Flak perhaps the deadliest antiaircraft weapon deployed by any combatant in World War II. The gun was mounted on a cruciform gun carriage. A simple-to-operate semi-automatic loading system ejected the fired shell; reloading involved simply inserting a new shell into a tray. The gun would fire and recoil; during the return stroke, the empty case was thrown backward by levers, after which a cam engaged and recocked the gun. The result was a firing rate of 15–20 rounds a minute, faster than similar weapons.

A battery consisted of four guns. Targeting indicators – either a Kommandogerät ("command device") fire control computer or a portable Würzburg radar that provided a remarkably high level of accuracy against aircraft – were attached to the central controller to each of the four guns of a battery, allowing for coordinated fire. Radar tracking was used to determine range and optical tracking for direction. With the automatic loading system, the gun layer's job was to keep the barrel trained on the target, based on the signals from the controller. The loaders would keep the weapon fed with live ammunition, which would fire immediately upon insertion, while the gun layer aimed the weapon according to the data.

Because the Germans did not possess proximity fuzes as the Allies did, observers were placed on the high mountain peaks to either side of the Brenner Pass, equipped with transits that allowed them to determine an attacking formation's altitude within

Würzburg radar folded for travel. This radar could be used for range-finding in place of the Kommandogerät. Antiflak measures included B-25s flying in advance of the bomber formation to drop "window," thin strips of aluminum foil to reflect the radar signal. The foil was very light and would stay aloft for quite some time. (Ekem/Wikipedia)

5ft. First Lieutenant Sterling Ditchey, a bombardier in the 310th Bomb Group, later recalled: "If the Germans had possessed proximity fuzes to use with their flak, we could never have flown these missions. They'd have blown us out of the sky!" The altitude at which the 88 was most accurate was 10,000ft, the exact altitude for most of the bombing missions.

The 88 was mounted on a cruciform gun carriage that was easily towed, the weapon's maneuverability only adding to its fearsome reputation. With their easy mobility, the Germans adopted the tactic of moving them around. Pilot Paul Young of the 321st Group recalled: "You'd approach a place where you'd been shot at on a previous mission, and begin to tighten up in expectation of running the gauntlet. Only there wouldn't be a single shot! Then, just as you relaxed, two or three would open up from a completely different position and scare the bejesus out of you worse than you'd been anticipating. It got to the point where I was just drum tight from the minute we crossed the bomb line till we flew back into Allied territory. That anticipation, the fear that built up – it took a lot out of you over the long run."

The second most important AA weapon over the Alps was the Flak 37, a medium antiaircraft weapon. In series production it was known as the 3.7cm Flak 18/36/37, and saw widespread service. The cannon was fully automatic and effective against aircraft flying at altitudes up to 15,700ft (4,785 meters), which put the 57th Wing's bombers well within range. It was produced in both towed and self-propelled versions. The original 37mm weapon was developed in 1935 by Rheinmetall as the 3.7cm Flak 18. The barrel had an overall length of 2.11 meters (89 caliber), which gave it the additional designation L/89. The original Flak 18 was produced in small numbers, with production ceasing in 1936. Continued development focused on replacement of the existing cumbersome dual-axle mount with a lighter single-axle version, resulting in the 3.7cm Flak 36 that appeared in 1937. The ballistic characteristics were unchanged, although the rate of fire was raised to 120rpm. A new, simplified sighting system introduced in 1938 resulted in the otherwise-identical 3.7cm Flak 37, which could be fired with great accuracy. These two versions were produced throughout the war.

During the final months of the war, a critical shortage of 88mm shells developed, and Luftwaffe units in Italy were limited to a total of 2,000 shells per day. Given that the Luftwaffe's own records showed that an average of 1,600 rounds were fired for each aircraft brought down, this put a severe crimp in the German ability to defend the Brenner rail line. It is not coincidental that the greatest destruction of the line came in late February, March, and April 1945.

Photo of Ala showing the positions of the German flak batteries during the war, some 3,000ft above the town. Mounting the guns this high on the hillsides meant that their shells would reach the bomber formations three seconds sooner than if they were located in the valley. This affected the evasive actions the bombers took after releasing their bombs. (57th Bomb Wing Archives, photo by Odorico Tonello)

Italian forces fought alongside the Germans in defending the Brenner lifeline. Their primary antiaircraft artillery piece was the Cannone da 90/53, a 90mm dual-purpose (antiaircraft/antitank) weapon designed and produced by Ansaldo, that was considered second only to the 88 in the antiaircraft role. The designation "90/53" meant that the gun had a 90mm caliber and a barrel length of 4.7 meters (53 caliber). The cannon could hit targets at altitudes up to 26,000ft (7,925 meters).

The first model of the Cannone da 90/53 commenced production in 1939. Originally, it was planned that the gun would be manufactured in three variants: 1,087 Modello 41Ps for static emplacement, 660 towable Modello 41Cs, and 57 mounted on heavy trucks designated Autocannoni da 90/53. However, Italian industry was not capable of producing these numbers of weapons, and by the time production ended in July 1943, only 539 guns in total had been delivered. Due to delays in producing adequate mounts, some were fitted on makeshift mounts on trucks such as the Lancia 3Ro and the Breda 52. After Italy surrendered, the Wehrmacht captured the majority of these guns, designating them the 9cm Flak 41(i) or 9cm Flak 309/1(i). Most were kept in service in Italy and were used to defend Verona. At the end of November 1944, the Germans moved 69 more 88s into the pass, giving them a total of 435 heavy weapons.

When clouds or smoke obscured the Mitchell formations, the Germans resorted to firing fixed barrages, though this was not considered as effective as visual aiming. However, the barrage was most fearsome to the

An example of the damage flak could do. This aircraft brought the crew home safely. Crews loved the B-25 for its rugged construction and resilience. (© Hymie Setzer Collection)

flyers who had to enter it. Dan Bowling, a lead pilot in the 321st Group, recalled: "A barrage looked like an exploding football field. When you saw that field of black explosions, you couldn't believe there was any way through it without being shot down. The 88 was the real killer, but when you saw a field of flak ahead where it was flickering with the rapid explosions from the 37s, the thought you were going to fly through that could scare the daylights out of you."

Most flak installations along the Brenner line were grouped into "*Grosse Batterien*," consisting of two or more heavy batteries at one location. These were installed around the centrally located fire control instruments. The latter usually consisted of two complete sets of equipment. The most important single feature inherent in a *Grosse Batterie* was that the two sets of fire control instruments made it possible to simultaneously track two different formations of aircraft, permitting control of the guns to be transferred rapidly from one formation to the other. In addition, these large flak sites provided concentrated firepower, and simplified repair, maintenance, supply, and administration. The greatest weakness of the *Grosse Batterien* was that they were a larger target for antiflak operations than was the case with independently sited batteries. For example, all 16 heavy guns at Rovereto were located at one site. After the site was successfully bombed by the antiflak flight, the 16 guns were split into two eight-gun batteries and positioned far enough apart that only one could be attacked at a time.

The Brenner terrain presented the flak units with difficulties that mirrored those of the attacking aircraft, there being only a few positions on the line where high mountains did not restrict fields of fire or interrupt radar reception. Because of this, it was impossible to place guns at San Michele, or to change the positions of defending guns at several other targets. The lack of gasoline for heavy movers and the amount of preparation needed to move and site a heavy battery properly were other factors which limited such movement.

By January 1945, flak positions had been identified in the mountains to either side of the pass at altitudes up to 3,000ft. One battery west of Ala was at 4,100ft, 3,000ft higher than the target. At Rovereto – known as the worst flak trap in Italy, where the bombers could only attack from one direction – the Germans put concrete gun pits halfway up the mountainsides in the narrow pass to either side of the town, only a few thousand feet below the bombers' altitude. In the positions at higher altitude in the mountains, the Germans sited both 88mm and 37mm weapons. German teams on the mountain tops equipped with transits were able to determine the altitude of the formations within 5ft, which improved the accuracy of the defenses.

Those guns sited near a target in a narrow valley had only a few moments to sight, aim, and fire their weapons at the bombers when they suddenly appeared overhead after crossing the mountains. When the German gunners already knew what direction they were coming from after receiving reports from other ground

In addition to the famous Krupp 88mm flak cannon, the Brenner Pass and Po Valley were also defended by smaller-caliber cannon such as the 3.7mm, which had a vertical range of 15,600ft and was thus easily able to reach the bombers normally flying at 10,000–12,000ft. (US Army)

An Italian Cannone da 90/53 mounted on a Lancia truck abandoned in North Africa. The 90mm gun was comparable to the Krupp 88mm cannon. It could fire 19 rounds per minute and had a vertical range of 39,000ft. (Australian War Memorial Collection)

stations, good crews could start firing in the right direction before the appearance of a formation, putting up a barrage field the attackers were forced to fly through.

In answer to these defenses, three antiflak planes would lead a formation, dropping strips of aluminum foil called "Window" to confuse the radar. In January 1945, an additional weapon was added: white phosphorus. When flak positions were spotted, the antiflak aircraft would attack with 100lb white phosphorous bombs to burn the gunners, damage the guns, and blow up the unused ammunition. The Germans considered use of white phosphorus to be chemical warfare, and announced that any captured bomber crews identified as having used white phosphorus would be summarily executed as war criminals. This happened to shot-down crews on at least three occasions between February 1945 and the end of the war.

Weather: a USAAF enemy

Weather often affected American missions during the winter of 1944/45. Conditions at the base, en route, and at the target were factors in the success of any given mission, and the weather usually differed between the three regions. Frequently, weather over Corsica would be good while that over the Brenner Pass and the areas they flew over might be poor or bad.

Cloud ceiling and cover were the major issues at Corsica, affecting the ability of the bombers to take off and return to their bases. Clouds south of the Po Valley had to either be overflown or diverted around so that the formation could fly over the mountains in clear skies. On reaching a safe altitude, it was necessary that no cloud layer have a solid top at 13,000ft or over because fully loaded B-25s began to strain at these altitudes, while aircrews also faced difficulty without additional oxygen.

On the other hand, the base of a complete overcast had to be 14,000ft or higher since the Alps ranged up to 10,000, 12,000, and even 15,000ft along the approaches to the targets.

A formation had to be able to top a cloud layer of 5/10 or more at 12,000ft. Over a Brenner target, it was necessary that cloud cover be no more than 5/10 if it were approximately 5,000ft below the formation, or 3/10 or less if it were nearer the altitude of the formation. Other weather factors that had the most influence on the success or failure of a mission were severe turbulence and heavy haze. With the passage of a cold or occluded front across the Alpine barrier, winds veer into the northerly quadrant and much dense air is banked up in southern Austria. The pressure gradient thus created between southern Austria and the Po Valley, augmented by the existing circulation, produces wind speeds across the mountains in excess of 40mph. These high winds coupled with the unevenness of the terrain set up large-scale eddy currents or turbulence, a significant hazard to aircraft, particularly those in formation.

The turbulence in the pass made flying difficult, and the potential for accidents was only a question of when they would happen. On January 21, 1945, Jerry Rosenthal of the 488th Squadron lost his friend Staff Sgt Aubrey Porter to a freak accident from the harsh conditions. As he recalled: "Our mission was to the Ora–San Michelle [*sic*] Railroad Diversion. Porter was tail gunner in '8P,' in the second box flying number three. There was very rough air over the target and the planes were bouncing violently with great fluctuations in altitude. We made three runs because the bombardiers couldn't get lined up and the flight leader was gung-ho. On the third run there was heavy, accurate flak. '8U' was number six, directly below '8P.' Just before bombs away, '8U' bounced up and struck the right tail section of '8P' with its left propeller, which cut away the right rudder and stabilizer and continued into the tail gunner's compartment and part of the left stabilizer. Porter was actually cut out of the tail! '8U' lost its left wing, fell into a flat spin and went down." The War Diary quoted the tail gunner in the lead ship: "Porter fell through space without a 'chute. I saw his 'chute and 8U's wing fall past us. There were no 'chutes from 8U."

The 340th Group's War Diary also reported: "Second Lieutenant William B. Pelton and his co-pilot, Flight Officer Harry K. Shackelford, pulled an aerodynamic miracle this afternoon when they brought their B-25 back without its right stabilizer or right elevator. How they landed the plane safely is still bewildering our operations officer and the hundreds of men who saw the damaged craft come in." The B-25 was rebuilt and continued to fly. The 321st Group's Paul Young recalled that mid-air collisions were his greatest fear: "There was a lot of clear air turbulence in the mountains, and you had no idea it was going to be a threat until suddenly you were in it. With flak, you could see it and thus be ready for it, or sometimes even take evasive action and avoid it, but turbulence was an invisible enemy."

Even when an airplane was on its own, the crews were forced to fight nature. Co-pilot 2nd Lieutenant Victor Hancock of the 445th Squadron recalled a mission where his plane was hit and dropped out of formation. The pilot turned away into what turned out to be a box canyon that was too narrow for them to turn around. Hancock recollected: "We were climbing against the downslope winds that were going down only a little bit slower than we were going up. We were holding maximum power and just barely climbing. All those rocks out in front of us

The Italian Alps are beautiful and rugged, but a difficult location for fighting a war, with extreme cold at altitude, unpredictable wind gusts coming off the mountains, and inhospitable terrain if you had to bail out. The B-25s were not equipped with oxygen, making hypoxia a constant concern. (57th Bomb Wing Archives, Edward Betts Collection)

ROVERETO   RAIL BR
A-698035   295°

A bombardier's view of the approach to Rovereto. After cresting the mountains, he had a very short time to lock on to the target. From this point, the bomber would be over the target in about three or four seconds. (57th Bomb Wing Archives)

definitely had my attention as we got closer and closer. In the end, we cleared the ridge by maybe 20 feet. That was my scariest mission and it didn't have anything to do with the Germans."

At the other extreme, a dry air mass over the Alps meant that winds dropped to calm, with resulting heavy haze, primarily concentrated close to the ground but at times extending to bombing altitude. When the haze was close to the ground, it could obscure the target too much for visual bombing, while if it was at higher altitudes, it made maintaining formation and navigation difficult. Light winds and the confinement of the atmosphere in the narrow valleys could exacerbate the haze. Additionally, these conditions helped the enemy when they deployed smoke pots to create additional haze.

The angle of the sun could also affect the success of a mission. For many of the targets in narrow valleys surrounded by high mountains, there were only a few hours in the day when the sun angle was such that the target could be seen outside the deep shadows of the mountains. Favorable weather for an attack was more important than sun angle, for the safety of the aircrews. This frequently meant that while a mission could get to a target, it could not take the best advantage of the good weather, since the bombardiers had trouble finding the target in time to make their drops successfully. Between November 6, 1944, and May 2, 1945, when the campaign ended, there were 118 days where the weather was acceptable. Successful missions were flown on 85 of those days. Between weather conditions, the natural difficulties of terrain, and the size of most of the targets, the Brenner Pass campaign was the most difficult operation of its kind undertaken by the US Army Air Forces during the war.

The unlucky 340th Bomb Group lost its entire fleet of aircraft on three separate occasions during the war. They first lost all 18 of their training aircraft due to a violent hail storm while still stateside. All aircraft were then lost due to the March 1944 eruption of Mount Vesuvius. Then in May 1944, the Luftwaffe destroyed nearly all of their aircraft on the ground during an early-morning raid. (57th Bomb Wing Archives)

CAMPAIGN OBJECTIVES
Endgame in the north of Italy

The Gothic Line

In early August 1944, the German armies arrived at the Gothic Line and settled in to the defenses Rommel had designed. The line was ten miles deep and extended from south of La Spezia on the west coast to the Foglia Valley, on through the natural defensive wall of the Apennines – a mountain range 50 miles deep with peaks rising to 7,000ft, covered with thick forest – to the Adriatic Sea between Pesaro and Ravenna on the east coast. The fortifications included concrete-reinforced gun pits and trenches, 2,376 machine-gun pillboxes with interlocking fire, 479 antitank, mortar, and assault gun positions' 390,000ft of barbed wire, and several miles of antitank ditches. All were positioned on steep hillsides that reduced combat to a small-unit infantry struggle.

By August, the total combined strength of the US Fifth and British Eighth armies had fallen precipitously from 249,000 to 153,000. The veteran infantry units were replaced by the inexperienced troops of the Brazilian Expeditionary Corps and the American 92nd Infantry Division. The total Allied force was reduced to only 18 divisions confronting the German Tenth and Fourteenth armies' 14 front-line divisions, backed up by between four and seven reserve divisions. Both the Fifth and Eighth armies were strong in armor but short on infantry, which put them at a disadvantage with their German opponents, considering the terrain they were to fight in. There would be no quick end to the bloodletting in Italy.

Railroad marshalling yards, a common target of the 57th Bomb Wing, were hit with great effect. The destruction of rail lines and bridges had a devastating effect on the enemy. After the war, Göring said: "The disruption of our communication lines has done more harm to us than the destruction of our factories." (57th Bomb Wing Archives, Edward Betts Collection)

The failure of Operation *Olive*

Operation *Olive*, the biggest battle ever fought in Italy, involving over 1.2 million troops on both sides, began on August 25, 1944. The battle plan called for the Eighth Army to attack up the Adriatic coast toward Pesaro and Rimini to draw in the German reserve divisions. At the same time, Fifth Army would attack the weakened central Apennines sector of the German lines north of Florence, striking toward Bologna, while the British XIII Corps on

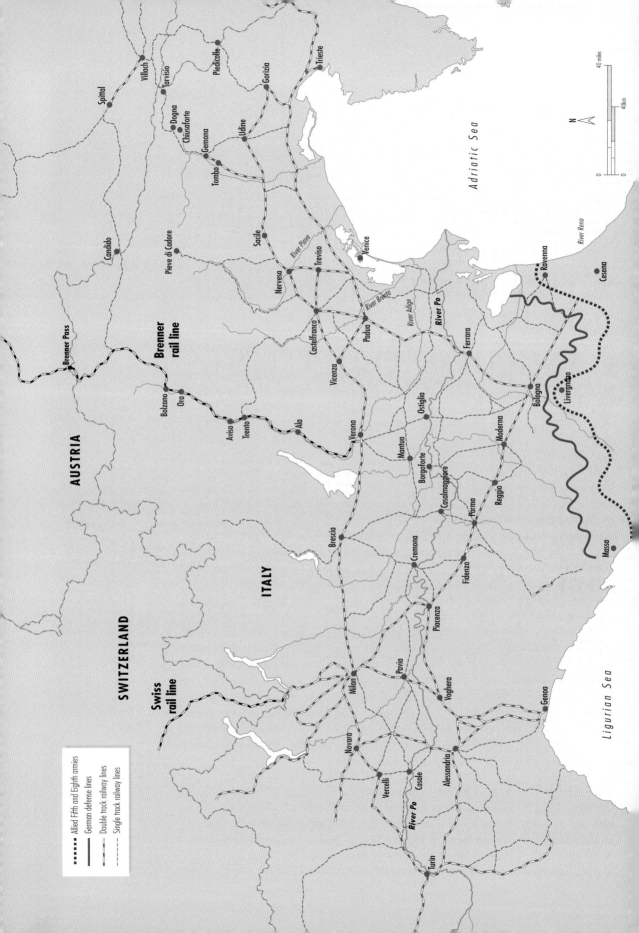

Map labels

Legend:
- ▪▪▪▪ Allied Fifth and Eighth armies
- ▬▬ German defense lines
- ━━ Double track railway lines
- --- Single track railway lines

Seas:
- Adriatic Sea
- Ligurian Sea

Countries:
- AUSTRIA
- SWITZERLAND
- ITALY

Rail lines:
- Brenner rail line
- Swiss rail line

Rivers:
- River Piave
- River Brenta
- River Adige
- River Po
- River Reno

Places:
Spittal, Villach, Tarvisio, Piedicolle, Gorizia, Trieste, Dogna, Chiusaforte, Gemona, Udine, Tomba, Candido, Pieve di Cadore, Sacile, Treviso, Venice, Nervesa, Castelfranco, Padua, Ferrara, Ravenna, Cesena, Vicenza, Bologna, Livergnato, Brenner Pass, Bolzano, Ora, Ostiglia, Moderna, Aviso, Trento, Ala, Verona, Mantua, Borgoforte, Casalmaggiore, Reggio, Parma, Massa, Brescia, Cremona, Fidenza, Piacenza, Milan, Pavia, Voghera, Genoa, Novara, Vercelli, Casale, Alessandria, Turin

OPPOSITE GOTHIC LINE AND RAILROADS IN NORTHERN ITALY 1944–45

the right wing advanced toward the Adriatic coast. The goal was to create a pincer with the Eighth Army advance to trap and destroy a major part of the German forces.

The initial British attack surprised the Germans, with General von Vietinghof away on leave and the LXVI Panzerkorps still pulling back its forward units to the main fortifications of the Gothic Line. Marshal Kesselring, unsure if this was a major offensive or only the British advancing to occupy vacated ground, with the main Allied attack to come on the Bologna front, refused to bring forward his reserves, as the Allied plan had hoped.

On August 28, a British officer who failed to destroy his detailed copy of Eighth Army commander Field Marshal Leese's order of attack was captured. Kesselring thus finally realized he faced a major offensive. By August 30, the Canadian I Corps and British V Corps reached the main defensive positions of the German first line of defense.

By September 3, they had advanced to the second line; the Canadians were close to breaking through to Rimini and the Romagna plain. However, V Corps' advance was slowed in the difficult mountain terrain with its poor roads. After two days of close-in fighting with heavy losses on both sides, the Allied assault was called off. An attack to outflank the ridge defenses by attacking the German position at Gemmano became known as "The Cassino of the Adriatic." Between September 4 and 13, the 56th Division and then the 46th Division made 11 unsuccessful assaults against Gemmano. On September 15, the Indian 4th Division made the 12th attack at 0300hrs and finally secured the German positions. The German 98th Division held Croce over five days of door-to-door and hand-to-hand fighting before the 56th Division forced their withdrawal.

On September 20, the Canadians broke through the German positions and moved onto the Lombardy Plain, while the 3rd Greek Mountain Brigade entered Rimini on the morning of September 21. At this point the weather changed for the worse, with the early onset of torrential autumn rains which turned the rivers into unbridgeable torrents and halted air operations. Movement slowed to a crawl and the open salient to the Lombardy Plain closed. In five weeks of fighting, Commonwealth losses were 14,000 men. The Eighth Army was fought out; Kesselring's dogged defense had won the day.

Throughout these battles, the 57th Bomb Wing was intimately involved as they went after German transport routes and bombed the bridges on the Po River to cut off the German front from Bologna, the central supply center at the southern end of the Brenner Pass. During a mission on September 10 to bomb the Guerra ammunition and fuel dump in support of the British, the 310th Group met the Italian pilots of the 2nd Grupo Caccia of the pro-German *Aeronautica Nazionale Repubblicana*. Despite their repeated attempts to break up the 310th Group formation, the Mitchells managed to hit the target successfully.

The US Fifth Army faced four divisions of the German Fourteenth Army which had settled into mountain fortifications that negated the use of armor in attack. The US II Corps and

The 57th Bomb Wing bombers appreciated the escorts from various fighter groups, including British Spitfires, the Tuskegee "Red Tails," and here, a P-51 Mustang from the 325th Fighter Group. (© Hymie Setzer Collection)

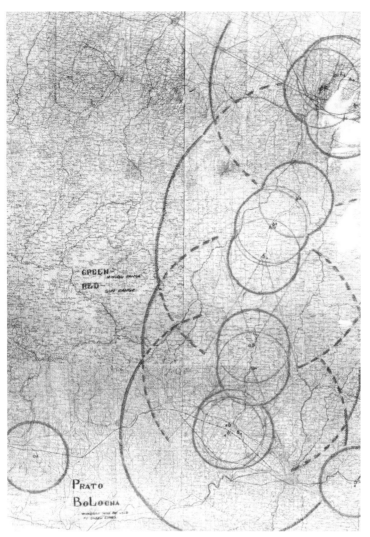

On this map of the area around Bologna, the large circles show the effective space for dropping chaff to confuse enemy radar tracking the bombers. The smaller circles show the range of the enemy antiaircraft guns. (57th Bomb Wing Archives, Edward Betts Collection)

British XIII Corps moved into the mountains, where German outposts provided fierce resistance, but following the withdrawal of three divisions to reinforce the Adriatic front, the Germans were forced to withdraw. Over five days of battle, the Fifth Army had finally fought their way to the main Gothic Line defenses. Between September 21 and October 3, the US 88th Division fought itself to a standstill on the route to Imola, losing 2,105 men killed and wounded, equaling the entire losses of the rest of II Corps in breaching the Gothic Line.

The II Corps renewed the offensive toward Bologna on October 5, supported by XIII Corps. Progress was gradual against stiffening opposition, and the attack came to a stop 20 miles from Bologna when the weather intervened as it had on the Adriatic front, closing air operations for 14 days. Air support was impossible due to rain and low clouds, while the rain turned the roads to the distant supply dumps near Florence into morasses. On Corsica, the men of the 57th Wing handed in their lightweight summer gear in favor of winter uniforms. Only a few missions were flown throughout October, with the majority that did get off the ground recalled due to bad weather. As the 321st Group's war diarist wrote: "A mission that was scrubbed for weather didn't count for your total to finish a tour. But try telling your mind and body that it didn't count!"

By the second half of October, it was clear that exhaustion and combat losses were increasingly affecting the Allied ground forces' ability to continue the offensive. On October 16, the Fifth Army made a last effort to take Bologna. The Allies in Italy were now short of artillery ammunition caused by a global reduction in production due to premature anticipation of imminent German defeat. Fifth Army's artillery was rationed to the point that the total rounds fired in the last week of October were less than that fired during one eight-hour period on October 2. Fighting on for the next 11 days, II Corps and XIII Corps made little progress toward Bologna. Unfortunately, the last four miles to Bologna were over difficult terrain and were defended by three of the best German divisions in Italy.

It was now clear that the buildup to full strength of the 1st Brazilian Division and reinforcement of the 92nd Division had not nearly compensated Fifth Army for the units sent to fight in France. The situation in the Eighth Army was worse: replacements were now diverted to northern Europe, while the Canadian I Corps had orders to prepare for shipment to the Netherlands in February 1945. Commonwealth losses in the war were now such that the ground units were reduced in strength by a third.

Throughout the operation, the bombers of the Mediterranean Allied Tactical Air Force had attacked the bridges over the Po River in an attempt to cut off the German forces south of the river from their supply points on the northern side. Conditions in the Po Valley campaign differed greatly from the interdiction campaign of Operation *Strangle*. In order to block traffic effectively, a dozen main lines and many alternate lines had to be cut. The Po and its tributary rivers were shallow and low-banked, which allowed easier repair and facilitated construction of diversions. Most importantly, by this time, the enemy had built up a large, efficient, and well-equipped repair organization which was capable of undertaking much more extensive repair and construction work than had been attempted previously.

The bombing attacks achieved considerable success in cutting east–west traffic, primarily by the repeated destruction of rail bridges crossing the north–south Po tributaries. However, blocking the north–south lines was more difficult since these bridges crossed the Po itself. Operation *Mallory Major*, which was carried out by the 57th and 42nd Bomb Wings, saw 23 Po River bridges destroyed or blocked during three days in early October. However, the Germans were able to construct diversionary pontoon bridges over the course of a week, and increased the antiaircraft defenses at these locations. When a rail line was cut, it forced the enemy to divert their limited available motor transport to carry the supplies around the cut, which in turn created a shortage in motor transport used for loading and unloading trains at their point of departure and destination.

There was only one bridge on the lower Brenner more than 135ft long, the one at Verona that was so heavily defended it could not be attacked. The ten remaining bridges crossed small streams feeding into the Adige River; they averaged 95ft in length and, with the exception of the Rovereto and Ala bridges, were squat, strong, masonry structures. The most frequently attacked target on the entire Brenner line was the Rovereto rail bridge, 12 miles south of Trento, which was subjected to a total of 21 attacks. The original 135ft parallel-span steel structure was destroyed in December 1944, and four replacement bridges

An example of the "Box Score" reconnaissance photos tracking the bomb fall and the accuracy of the bombers. Note the massive number of bomb craters around the target, a sign of previous bombings. These targets were hit multiple times due to the German engineers' amazing ability to rebuild. (57th Bomb Wing Archives)

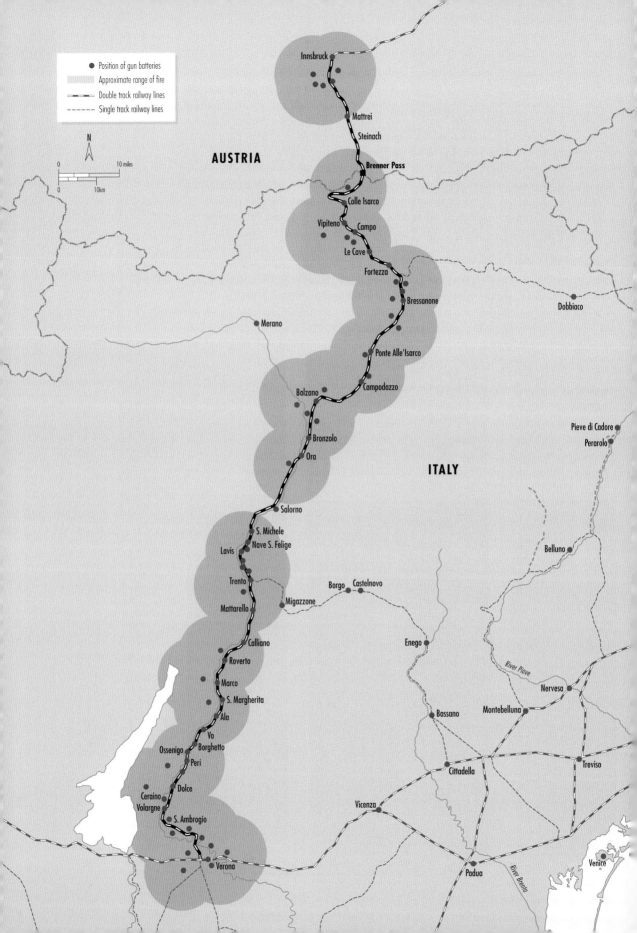

Position of gun batteries
Approximate range of fire
Double track railway lines
Single track railway lines

N

0   10 miles
0   10km

AUSTRIA

Innsbruck

Mattrei

Steinach

Brenner Pass

Colle Isarco

Vipiteno   Campo

Le Cave

Fortezza

Bressanone

Dobbiaco

Merano

Ponte Alle'Isarco

Campodazzo

Bolzano

Bronzolo

Ora

Pieve di Cadore

Perarolo

ITALY

Salorno

S. Michele
Nave S. Felige

Lavis

Belluno

Trento

Borgo   Castelnovo

Mattarello

Migazzone

River Piave

Calliano

Enego

Roverto

Marco

Nervesa

S. Margherita

Ala

Bassano

Montebelluna

Vo

Borghetto

Ossenigo

Peri

Treviso

Ceraino

Dolce

Volargne

S. Ambrogio

Cittadella

Vicenza

Verona

Enego

Padua

River Brenta

Venice

OPPOSITE THE GUNS OF THE BRENNER PASS

This map shows the disposition of German defenses in the Brenner Pass in March 1945. The range of fire of over 500 heavy antiaircraft guns covered nearly every square inch of the pass.

were subsequently destroyed. In addition, the replacement bridges were damaged on several missions, with the line blocked for periods of up to a week. The 120ft Ala bridge was attacked 24 times and destroyed on seven missions. Despite the fact that the bridges were extremely short, experience proved, as had been anticipated, that they were more profitable as interdiction targets than fills or cuts. While these bridges could be replaced in two to five days, they created longer cuts than the easily repaired fills or marshalling yards.

By late October, the German defenses around Monte Castello, Monte Belvedere, Della Toraccia, Castelnuovo di Vergato, Torre di Nerone, La Serra, Soprassasso, and Castel D'Aiano still held. The onset of winter meant there would be no breakthrough against the revitalized German defenses. Supplies of Allied artillery ammunition, food, and mechanized equipment could not be brought forward in sufficient quantities over mountain roads clogged with mud and ice. The terrain was cut up into innumerable small segments by a fine network of rivers and canals which were subject to fall and winter flood, in addition to artificial flooding on the part of the Germans that made these waterways into raging torrents that kept the normally dry fields in a swamp-like condition. The Allied ground forces met determined resistance that was at least as strong as their offensive power; this equality of forces meant the advantage now lay with the enemy.

With the onset of winter rains that turned to snow in the mountains, the Allied troops settled in for a miserable existence on mountainous front lines in what would be the coldest European winter in a century. With the mountain roads now covered with ice and snow, the Allied armies were forced to go over to an "aggressive defensive" posture, with active patrolling and shelling of German positions to keep pressure on the enemy. From November 1, 1944, until April 9, 1945, there was no offensive action possible along the Gothic Line.

On November 1, 1944, the Southeastern Front Quartermaster General reported that the German armies in the Gothic Line were receiving 24,000 tons of supplies – 600 percent of their minimum daily requirements – shipped from Munich and Augsburg by rail through the Brenner Pass to Bologna, the main German supply hub. Even after bombing missions had been flown against the rail line over the summer, a train from Augsburg still took less than 12 hours to arrive in Bologna on most days. So long as this situation continued, Marshal Kesselring's promise to Hitler that his forces could hold out in northern Italy "indefinitely" would be made good. Now that large-scale offensive operations were impossible until the spring thaw that would come to the Alps in April 1945, some way had to be found over the intervening winter months to reduce enemy strength.

Polesella Pontoon Bridge

In July 1944, executing Operation *Mallory Major*, the 57th Bomb Wing destroyed all 22 steel bridges over the Po River in northern Italy. Nevertheless, German engineers did an excellent job of building pontoon bridges and using ferries to continue supplying their troops.

With the collapse of the Gothic Line, the 57th Bomb Wing was charged with making an all-out effort to destroy those crossings and trap the German forces in Italy below the Po River, often flying three missions per day.

On April 22, 1945 the 321st Bomb Group sent 12 bombers to take out the pontoon bridge at Polesella. The weather was good with only 3/10 cloud cover and 10-mile visibility. The bridge was well defended: flak was heavy caliber, moderate, and accurate; 11 of the B-25s were holed by enemy antiaircraft fire. In spite of the resistance, aircraft from the 446th Bomb Squadron hit the bridge with pinpoint accuracy.

The 57th Wing's operations were so effective that many of the retreating German soldiers had to swim across the Po River to escape the advancing Allied ground troops, leaving behind their heavy weapons.

Starving the Gothic Line with air power

With the armies unable to operate effectively on the Italian mainland during the coming winter, only airpower would be able to reduce the German supplies. General Knapp put his 57th Bomb Wing planning section to work to devise a plan of attack.

The most famous and important of the passes through the Alps that separate Austria from northern Italy, the Brenner Pass is also the lowest, with a maximum elevation of 4,511ft (1,375 meters). It has always been important militarily, since it can be kept open in the winter without undue hardship. Before there were roads, the Brenner was the primary invasion route from the north into Italy; Hannibal's elephants passed through it in 218 BC. Until a carriage road was constructed in 1777 at the behest of Empress Maria Theresa of Austria, the road was a track for mule trains and carts. The railway was completed in 1867, and is the only transalpine rail route without a major tunnel.

The main line of supply for the German armies in northern Italy came through the Brenner Pass, with some additional supply through Switzerland. In July 1944, Operation *Mallory Major* was launched to destroy all of the bridges over the Po River to stop the flow of supplies from the rail lines north of the river. The German engineers were so good at building pontoon bridges and ferrying supplies across the river, that the Allies were forced to turn their efforts to destroying the rail traffic north of the Po Valley.

Of all the rail communications lines used by the enemy, the most important was the line through the Brenner Pass. Three rail lines funneled supplies, equipment, and troops from Germany into the northern terminus of the line at Innsbruck in Austria for passage into Italy. The most important of the three feeder routes was the double-track line from the northeast, running along the Inn River from Munich and Augsburg. The second passed through the mountains direct from Munich, and the third ran east from Lake Constance. All three of these lines were fed in turn by the complex Austrian and southern German rail systems. From Innsbruck, the line ran south through the Alps to Verona, ten miles east of the southern tip of Lake Garda. The southern terminus of the Brenner Pass line was Verona, from where rail lines fanned out east, west, and south into the Po Valley. The main lateral line ran west to Milan and Turin and east to Vincenza, from where three single-track lines went south to the Po and the battlefields south of the river in the Appenines.

Even when operating at a fraction of normal capacity, the double-track Brenner line was capable of fully supplying all the needs of the German armies in Italy. At the height of its traffic, 72 trains carrying German troops and supplies passed south over this route each day. Verona, the southern terminus of the Brenner line, was the center of the largest concentration of military installations and dumps in Italy. Some 30 factories, ammunition, fuel, and general stores dumps, and motor transport depots, all fed by the Brenner line, were located there.

The Germans were fortunate that the Brenner Pass rail line was electrified, which meant they did not have to use their steam locomotives and thus divert dwindling coal supplies to Italy. However, if the line's

The railroad bridge at Rovereto was the most attacked bridge on the Brenner line, receiving 27 attacks. It was only 135ft long, and after the original bridge was destroyed, the 57th Bomb Wing had to return time and again to destroy four replacement bridges. (57th Bomb Wing Archives)

electrical power could be destroyed, the Germans would be forced to replace the electric locomotives with steam. With the German rail system across Europe under attack in 1944/45, this would add further pressure on Germany's transport problems – and some of the trains' cargo capacity would have to be used for coal to power the replacement locomotives. The Allied planners determined that if electric power could be cut, it would reduce the carrying capacity of the line to 6,740 tons a day, since the Germans did not possess sufficient steam engines to divert them to Italy to replace the Brenner electric engines one-for-one. While this was still close to 200 percent of their minimum daily requirement, there would be little margin for error on the part of the Germans.

Once the number of trains was reduced, the bombers would be sent against the marshalling yards and stations along the line, all 24 of its bridges, the storage areas, and the repair depots. The campaign would be a race against the German repair units, requiring multiple missions to a target even once it had been hit hard enough to knock it out, so that it would remain out of action. If German repairs were delayed or prevented, the Gothic Line could be cut off over the course of the winter.

On October 20, General Knapp presented his plan for Operation *Bingo* to his old friend Ira Eaker, with whom he had served on the Mexican border after World War I. Eaker, now commander of the Mediterranean Allied Air Forces, saw the promise in Operation *Bingo*. The USAAF could starve the Gothic Line over the winter, leaving it weakened enough for the ground forces to attack in the spring and bring the war in Italy to a rapid end. Eaker sent the plan on to Mediterranean theater commander General Sir Harold Alexander, who approved Knapp's proposal on October 23.

The campaign would commence on Monday, November 6, 1944. The first priority targets were the electrical transformer stations between Verona and Bolzano. There were 14 of these electrical transformers, situated 10–20 miles apart, depending on the rail line grade. To cut electric power over any section, it was necessary to destroy at least three consecutive stations, since the system could still operate at reduced capacity if only two stations had to be bypassed.

All this would be carried out by a medium bomber force that would be cut in half in comparison with the forces available during the summer months, with the 42nd Bomb Wing transferred to France at the end of November and the 319th Bomb Group withdrawn from Italy and returned to the United States in January 1945. For the final and most difficult part of the air campaign, only the three bomb groups remaining in the 57th Wing would be available.

The importance of the Brenner bridges

Once the electrical power was knocked out, the campaign would move on to target the rail line itself. The essential purpose of attacks on the Brenner line was to interdict traffic, not to destroy rolling stock or rail facilities. Supplies coming over the Brenner Pass from Innsbruck were consigned directly to destinations in Italy, and no marshalling or break-down of trains was required north of Verona. Thus, attacks on marshalling yards delayed the movement of traffic for only as long as it took to repair a single line through the yard. As the Germans always had sufficient rolling stock to carry essential freight, the destruction of the rolling stock itself contributed only in delaying the repair of track. Rail yards were seldom congested, but a few of the precious steam engines and repair facilities were destroyed or damaged. As the battle for the Brenner progressed, and attacks were pushed further north, valuable shipments of equipment and supplies were being isolated between the cuts. This forced the Germans to keep trains in marshalling yards or disperse them along the track. Some yards were quite small, so as few as 150–300 units of rolling stock filled them to 75 percent capacity. When the yards became congested, they were attacked both to interdict traffic further and to destroy valuable supplies.

An unidentified rail bridge in northern Italy that fell victim to the USAAF bombers. These photos show clearly how devastating a bomb load on target could be. (57th Bomb Wing Archives)

The greatest difficulty was the lack of suitable targets. Guided by prior experience, it was known that to create lasting breaks in the rail line it would be necessary to destroy bridges. Long-term cuts were essential during winter weather which canceled operations for days at a time. Damage to marshalling facilities, tunnels, open track, fills, and cuts could be repaired quickly and easily. However, there were only eight bridges 200ft or more in length on the Brenner line. Bolsano, Ora, San Michele, and Lavis were already bypassed by diversions. The fifth bridge, at Verona, was so strongly protected with antiaircraft guns that it was not considered profitable to attack. Campobasso, the sixth, could not be bombed due to terrain difficulties. The remaining two, the Bressanone and Vipiteno bridges, were defended by large concentrations of heavy antiaircraft guns following the first successful strikes, making them uneconomical targets.

This lack of long, vulnerable bridges forced attention to small bridges, some only 40–60ft long. Targets of this size demanded the most accurate pinpoint bombing, and their low, short-span construction made repairs or building of bypasses relatively easy for the repair crews. Fills were attacked and marshalling yards bombed when the more important yards were clogged with backed-up rolling stock. The same effort was directed against landslides, tunnel-mouths, and cuts, with unsatisfactory results. Fortunately, the best results of the entire campaign were achieved at the outset against three transformer stations.

The targets of Operation *Bingo*

The Brenner railway was standard-gauge, electrified, and double-tracked throughout its 168 miles. Regarding targets, the line can be divided into three sections: the lower Brenner from Verona to Trento, the middle Brenner from Trento to Bolzano, and the upper Brenner from Bolzano to Innsbruck.

Lower Brenner

On the lower Brenner section, the line ran from Verona north to Trento along the steep-sided Adige Valley on the east bank of the river. At points where the heavily wooded Alpine foothills rise abruptly from the river's edge, the rail line ran along fills at the bottom of the steep slopes; where the valley is wider, the line often left the river and ran in the shadow of the mountains half a mile distant. There were places where, within two miles of the line, the hills rose to 4,000ft above the track level. At Trento, a secondary single-track line branched southeast to join the lateral Udine–Vicenza–Verona line, 40 miles away at Cittadella. This route was seen as a possible effective alternate to the lower section, but only a comparatively small effort was required to keep it blocked. Attacks were carried out against 38 individual targets in the lower Brenner, including 10 rail bridges, 14 fills, three transformer stations, three possible landslides, two tunnel entrances, and one cut. Fifty percent of the total number of 57th Wing's attacks – 186 missions – were carried out against these targets during the entire campaign.

The lower Brenner offered a large number of fills or embankments that carried the track over low ground; 14 of these were attacked. The fills varied from a few hundred feet to several thousand feet in length, and in places were 20–30ft high. The best fill targets proved to be those closest to the river, such as those at Marco, Dolce, and Ossenigo, where water conditions hindered repair. The greatest weight of bombs fell on the Ossenigo rail fill, which was attacked seven times. However, fills continued to be considered as secondary in importance, to be attacked only when the bridge targets were already cut or blocked or when it seemed advisable to temporarily halt attacks on heavily defended bridges.

North of San Ambrogio, ten miles northwest of Verona, the rail line passed under a series of 300ft high limestone cliffs. This formation had been weakened through water action in a stratum along its base. According to reports by geologists of the Italian railroad association, two dangerous rocks, each several hundred cubic meters in volume, were displaced as a result of

ALDENO RAIL FILL A-762115
107°

Like many of the targets in the Brenner Pass, there was only one practical direction from which to make a bombing run on Aldeno. This was a great help to the crews of the Axis antiaircraft batteries. Target approaches also had to take into consideration the position of the sun, as the high mountains could put the targets in the shade before or just after midday. (57th Bomb Wing Archives)

subsidence and had long been in danger of collapsing onto the railroad below, and the Italian government had taken action to prevent such an event. The 57th Wing's B-25s made eight attacks with three different aiming points along this formation to try to create a landslide. Though the tracks were cratered, only an insignificant amount of rubble was brought down. Attacks on the tunnel at San Ambrogio just north of the landslide target were also unsuccessful; the limestone formation appeared too sturdy to be dislocated by 1,000lb bombs.

Many targets were nestled against hillsides in deep, V-shaped valleys. Frequently the target was visible only three or four miles from the bomb release point, making it essential the aircraft made the bomb run exactly on course. In the few seconds available, the bombardier had to pick up the small, shadow-covered target, make necessary corrections, and release bombs.

Rail communications in the Brenner region could be divided geographically into three parts. The first was the three parallel lines running northeast across the Venetian plain. Most important and first in priority for repair was the double-track Vicenza–Casarsa–Udine rail line. To the south of the main route was the single-track Piazzola–Treviso–Motta di Livenza line, and still further south the double-track Padua–Mestre–Latisana–Monfalcone line. It would be necessary to cut all three lines to interdict traffic. Flat terrain, low river banks, shallow streams, and short-span, low-silhouette bridges made repairs and construction of diversions relatively easy. Seven of the ten major bridges that had been destroyed during the Operation *Olive* bombings were now bypassed by diversion bridges that made it necessary to cut two bridges to create one block in any of the lines. There were, however, several long bridges, of which only a few were protected by flak.

The second, middle sector was the northeastern frontier between Italy and Austria, which included three of the four frontier routes available to the enemy. In order of importance, these routes were the Tarviso, the Postumia, and the Piedicolle routes. In December, the campaign was extended to this zone, northeast of the Venetian plain, to cut the enemy rail lines at points where repairs and construction of diversions would be difficult. Though the surrounding terrain imposed moderate difficulties on the attackers, there were several high, long-span bridges on each line. With these bridges knocked out, the use of the rail line by the enemy would be very difficult. In the event, the 120ft high Borovnica rail viaduct on the Postumia route was bombed on December 27, 1944, and one span was destroyed. The Germans were forced to attempt to construct a long, difficult diversion, which was not completed when the line was overrun by Marshal Tito's forces in April 1945. A single span of the Piedicolle route was blocked on December 31 by the destruction of a single span of the Canale d'Isonzo bridge ten miles north of Gorizia. The bridge was passable for only a few days late in January and early in February. This bridge, as well as that at Dogna five miles northeast which was cut in February, remained impassable until the cessation of hostilities.

Trento to Bolzano

North of Trento, the valley floor widens slightly as the line runs north to Bolzano. The mountains rise steeply from the valley floor; in places 8–10 miles from the river, they tower over 10,000ft. Sixteen targets were attacked in this section of the line, including nine bridges, five fills, and two marshalling yards. Unlike the lower Brenner, this section

The 488th Bomb Squadron's 8P, following a horrific midair collision due to turbulence over the Alps. The ship that struck this aircraft, 8U, went down with all crew lost. The tail gunner of 8P was 'chewed' out of his compartment and never found. All were amazed that the pilots were able to bring this aircraft back to base. (57th Bomb Wing Archives)

offered few small bridges or fills. The greatest problem confronting the interdiction plan was the construction of three diversions, which offered alternate routes for half the distance of the main line between Trento and Bolzano. On the main line between the diversions there were no targets of importance, thus making it necessary to block both the main line and the primary diversion lines.

Five miles north of Trento, the 3,000ft long, 35-span, masonry Lavis viaduct carried the tracks across the Avisio River. This target was attacked seven times and spans were destroyed on four occasions. The viaduct was bypassed by a two-mile diversion; the 90ft and 170ft bridges on the diversion were attacked 21 times, blocked on several occasions, and destroyed three times. The

P-47s from the 350th Fighter Group escort the 340th Bomb Group bombers on the March 16, 1945, mission to Brixlegg in Austria. (© Hymie Setzer Collection)

viaduct and the diversion had to be destroyed or damaged repeatedly as the enemy made an effort to keep both serviceable. At San Michele all'Adige, eight miles north of Trento, the track crossed to the west bank of the Adige River; 15 miles further north at Ora, it recrossed to the east bank. Two of the best targets were the 350ft steel bridges over the Adige at Ora and San Michele. However, both these bridges, as well as several smaller bridges on this section of the main line, were bypassed by the 15-mile Ora–San Michele diversion on the east bank of the river. Construction of the diversion by 5,000 men was completed on December 5, 1944, which made it necessary to block both the diversion and the main line. There were only two short bridges on the diversion. A total of 48 attacks were carried out against the diversion, 24 against the 120ft San Michele diversion bridge, and 12 against a short fill at Salorno. The third diversion bypassed a large bridge just south of Bolzano, where two cuts would have to be made, but due to a heavy flak concentration in the area, these targets were never attacked.

Bolzano to Innsbruck

The rail line north to the Brenner Pass summit had a difficult section, running northeast from Bolzano up the narrow Isarco River valley, where it crossed the river at several points and passed through several tunnels and under avalanche hoods. At Aica, a single-track line branched east, crossing into Austria near Sillian, where it joined the main line running north from Villach at Spittal. At Brennero, the line crossed the Alpine watershed, 4,600ft above sea level, and entered Austria. From that point it descended downhill through the Sill River valley to the narrower confined end of the valley before reaching Innsbruck, 22 miles north.

The problem of terrain became severe on the upper Brenner. An attacking formation had to pick their way through mountainous areas where the snow-covered peaks reached 12,000–13,000ft above sea level. The targets were practically hidden in the deep shadow-filled valleys, and a successful mission required the greatest skill on the part of the combat crews. Forty-three attacks were carried out against 11 bridges, three marshalling yards, two fills, and a tunnel. Sixteen of these attacks were against the 90ft bridges at Steinach and Matrei in Austria, and seven against the 150ft bridges at Campo in Italy. The best targets were on the upper Brenner. There were four 200ft bridges and none could be bypassed. The two bridges at Vipiteno and Bressasone were the only ones not hidden in steep valleys, but the flak defenses at both were strong. Thus, the majority of missions were flown against smaller, more difficult-to-hit targets that were not so well-defended.

In the six months of Operation *Bingo*, the 57th Bomb Wing's B-25s attacked 70 different rail targets on the 168 miles of track between Verona and Innsbruck. A total of 370 individual attacks were carried out.

THE CAMPAIGN
The hard last winter of the war

First missions

On March 20, 1945, the 340th Bomb Group flew its 800th mission of the war. Here, aircraft of the 488th Bomb Squadron are heading to bomb the railroad bridge at Pizzighettone. The 486th Bomb Squadron flying with them would lose one aircraft to flak. On the same day, the 488th lost two bombers over Campo. It was a bad day: no one was in the mood to celebrate the 800th mission. (Hymie Setzer Collection)

There were no thoughts of "Sunny Italy" during the winter of 1944/45, the coldest European winter in a century. Paul Young, who joined the 445th Squadron two weeks before Operation *Bingo* began, remembered: "We boarded up the tents as best we could, and we would supplement the coal ration by going out in search parties to cut down trees for fuel. A lot of the guys made stoves that burned avgas. We were cold on the ground, we were cold in the planes. I was just cold all the time." Young particularly recalled the night before Operation *Bingo*'s first mission, which was also his first mission: "It was cold and damp, which made it hard to sleep through the night in our tents without waking up shivering. Coupled with the fact I had the jitters for my first mission, I had no trouble getting up when they woke us at 0500 hours to get ready."

The target was the three main transformers on the lower Brenner line. The 310th Bomb Group was assigned to hit the transformers at San Ambrogio, while the 340th and 321st Bomb Groups would hit those at Trento and Ala respectively. If these strikes were successful, electrical power would be denied to trains as far north as Bolzano.

Captain Gerald Wagner led the nine B-25s of the 445th Squadron in "Vicious Vera," while Young was assigned as co-pilot for 2nd Lieutenant Max Poteete in "Val." The commander of the 446th Squadron, Lt Colonel Paul Cooper, led nine planes of his squadron, while 1st Lieutenant Marion Walker led nine from the 447th in "Cover Girl." Captain Harold Farwell led the 448th Squadron's nine in "Out of Bounds." All were loaded with eight 500lb HE bombs.

The transformer itself was a small target, and required real skill to take it out. With no flak or fighters over the target, each squadron's lead bombardier was able to zero in perfectly on the buildings. Indeed, the group's war diarist recorded afterwards that the concentrations were so good it was "pickle barrel bombing," with 100 percent of all bombs falling on the target. The Ala transformer was knocked out so thoroughly that it was not replaced until a new one was built after the war.

The 340th Bomb Group achieved equally good results at Trento, as did the 310th at San Ambrogio. As predicted, the power outage affected trains as far north as Bolzano, and within days Ultra had picked up reports of a drop in delivery to the predicted 10,000 tons, as well as orders to divert coal-fired locomotives from elsewhere to the Brenner line. Operation *Bingo* was off to a roaring start.

The next day, the campaign against the bridges began. The 321st Group hit the Sacile railroad bridge, putting a string of "thousand-pounders" right through the center to chalk up a 97.2 percent success mission, while the Motta di Livenza rail bridge's center span broke away and fell into the river, despite the fact the 5/10 cloud cover prevented six Mitchells of the 18 sent from dropping their loads.

After three days of strong winds on Corsica that kept flying to a minimum and bad weather over northern Italy, Friday, November 10, saw the first bad losses of the campaign,

The Ala railroad electric power generating station in the aftermath of Operation *Bingo*. The power station remained out of action for the remainder of the war, and the Germans had to divert steam engines to the Brenner rail line. (57th Bomb Wing Archives)

Donald C. Spalinger

On February 13, 1945, 12 B-25s from the 486th Bomb Squadron headed for San Ambrogio in the Brenner Pass intending to bomb a rocky mountain outcrop that would precipitate a landslide, blocking the main road. It was cold, but other than a ground haze the weather was clear.

The P-47s from the 66th Squadron, 57th Fighter Wing, escorted the bombers. When enemy fighters failed to appear, the P-47s switched their job to flak suppression.

Second Lt Donald C. Spalinger led the flight of fighters, diving on the gun positions in the hope of silencing them, or at least distracting them from targeting the bomber formation. He dove right down the throat of the guns, released his bombs, and pulled out of the dive.

His wingman 2nd Lt George M. Blackburn, following him in, saw white smoke trailing from Spalinger's "jug." He radioed to him, "Bail out! Bail out!" but received no reply. Now flames were streaming from the engine. The fighter continued to climb until it stalled out; dropping crazily off the left wing, it fell out of the sky.

The bombers plastered the mountain with bombs, but the mountain refused to budge so the main road through San Ambrogio remained clear. Two of the B-25s from the 486th Bomb Squadron failed to return to base. The mission was a complete failure.

"Position to Assume while over Target"

Sensible advice for aircrew. (57th Bomb Wing Archives)

with the 321st Group suffering at the hands of flak gunners. All four squadrons managed to put up a total of 44 Mitchells to bomb the temporary rail bridge and ferry terminal at Ostiglia that the German repair crews had recently completed. The bridge was fiercely defended and flak accounted for the bombers flown by two formation leaders and two other B-25s, and damaged a total of 30 planes.

The 446th Squadron lost the second element lead aircraft when it was hit in the right engine moments before reaching its target. Pilot 1st Lieutenant Walton Ligon was hit by a piece of shrapnel that almost amputated his left arm above the elbow. Co-pilot Captain Gale Dickson took over while bombardier 1st Lieutenant Lawrence Clausen applied a tourniquet to Ligon. When the B-25 took a second hit, Dickson ordered the crew to bail out. Clausen, navigator 1st Lieutenant John Chapman, radioman Tech Sergeant Julius Nagy, and tailgunner Staff Sergeant George Glendening got out, but the two pilots went down with the bomber and turret gunner Staff Sergeant Vernon Bender's parachute failed to open. Nagy and Clausen were rescued by partisans, while the others were caught and became POWs. The other 11 bombers were damaged by the intense flak, with crewmen wounded in each.

The 447th Squadron also took heavy losses. Mission leader "Ready Teddie," flown by Captain Maurice "Wigs" Wiginton, was hit in both main gas tanks but only one sealed. Flak knocked out the electrical system and fumes from the ruptured tank overcame bombardier 1st Lieutenant Leeland Messna, preventing a drop. Wiginton was able to land "Ready Teddie" back at Solenzara despite a full bomb load.

Bursts of flak around the tail and the belly of 9X, far too close for comfort. Crews could smell the gunpowder as they flew through flak, and sometimes feel the concussion of a near miss. Most unnerving was the rattle of shrapnel as it rained down on the thin aluminum skin of the aircraft. (57th Bomb Wing Archives)

Two more B-25s from the third and fourth formations were also lost, while all the others were hit by flak; four crewmen were killed and 12 injured. Just as "Desirable," the 448th Squadron's lead ship flown by 1st Lieutenant Douglas Anderson, reached the Initial Point – the point before an aircraft began its bomb run – flak destroyed the left engine. Anderson continued on; the hydraulic system was knocked out and the landing gear and flaps came down. Another burst near the cockpit covered the pilots with shattered plexiglass and cut a rudder control cable. Douglas managed to stay airborne for 20 minutes until their passage was blocked by tall mountains they couldn't fly around. The crew parachuted safely, and all but Douglas – who was captured – were rescued by partisans and returned to Corsica in December.

In all, 32 aircrew were killed or wounded, one of the heaviest losses of any mission. Despite the opposition, the 321st knocked out seven spans of the pontoon bridge. Paul Young remembered: "It was my first mission where the Germans made a serious attempt to kill me. It wasn't easy to sit there as co-pilot and take it as all that flak exploded around us, but in retrospect it was better I had that first experience as a co-pilot where I wasn't responsible for a crew while I put everything I'd heard other people say about how to control fear to work."

Winter closes in

The weather favored the enemy in the period between late November and late December. Many missions were canceled throughout December as winter weather delivered rain and wet snow on Corsica; on half the days when the weather was good enough to launch a mission from the island, the weather over the mainland was so bad the strike force was called back or aborted when their leaders found the targets cloud-covered. Each group began to send weather reconnaissance flights in the morning to see the mainland weather for themselves in an attempt to get in missions wherever possible.

The Brenner rail line was open on December 1. The next day, the bridges at Ala, Rovereto, and Calliano on the lower Brenner were attacked, while San Michele on the middle Brenner was hit. Ground haze and generated smoke obscured the targets at San Michele, Calliano, and Rovereto, and each strike was met with heavy, intense flak. Though none of the bridges were destroyed, damage was enough to close the line for two days, though it reopened on December 5. Missions were canceled due to weather until December 10, when four bridges, two fills, and two potential landslides on the lower Brenner were attacked. Two B-25s were shot down and ten were struck by flak. Again, the weather closed in and no missions could be mounted until December 26. That day, the wing struck the bridges at Rovereto and Calliano, a fill at Dolce, and a potential landslide at San Ambrogio, cutting the line at all four locations. On the 27th, the Calliano and Rovereto bridges were hit again, and a tunnel entrance at San Ambrogio.

On December 27 and 28, heavy bombers of the XV Air Force struck the marshalling yards at Innsbruck. Over the last three days of the month, B-25s went after the lower Brenner, hitting the bridges at Calliano, San Margherita, and Ala, and a long section of fill at Dolce. The Lavis viaduct in the middle Brenner was hit on December 31. Despite all this, the middle and upper Brenner were still open at the end of the month. Overall, the Brenner line was only cut on 12 days during December. The end of 1944 saw the weather improve, which would continue through most of January as Italy became clear and very cold. January and February would see a total of 46 operational days.

A change of command helps Allied fortunes

As the 57th Bomb Wing continued its engagement in the battle over the Brenner, change came to the Italian theater at the end of 1944. In December, vainglorious Fifth Army commander General Mark Clark was appointed to command the 15th Army Group as

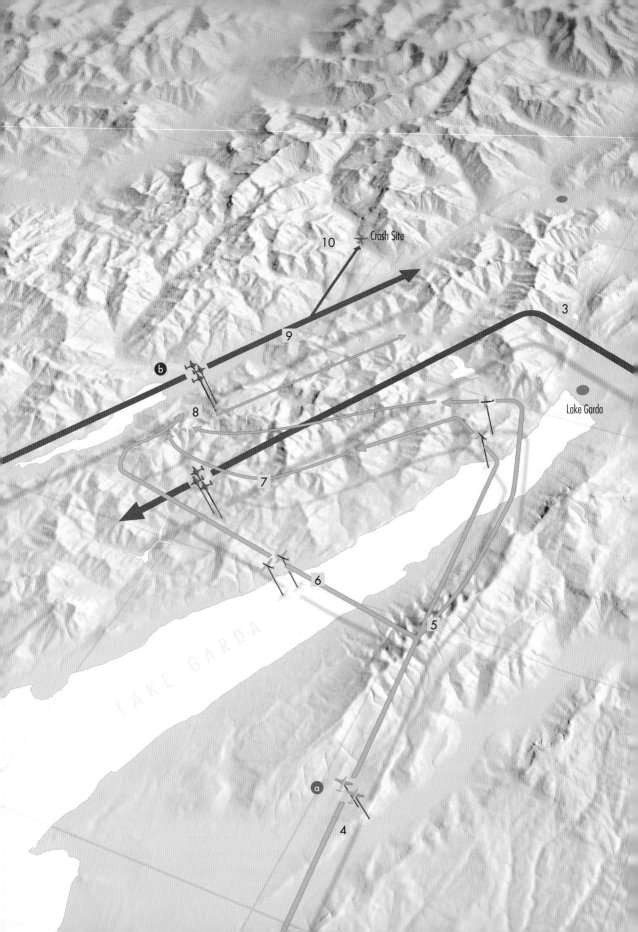

10

Crash Site

3

9

b

8

Lake Garda

7

6

5

LAKE GARDA

a

4

December 10, 1944 Over the Brenner Pass

EVENTS

1 A formation of 17 B-25 bombers of the 340th Bombardment Group, 488th Bomb Squadron make their final course adjustment, turning on to the bomb run over the Initial Point, the town of Arsiero.

2 The last box of six aircraft take heavy fire from the German guns at Rovereto. "Tail End Charlie," the last ship in the formation, gets hit by flak, knocking the camera out of the tail gunner's hands.

3 Clear of the German 88mm antiaircraft guns, the formations turn for home just west of Lake Garda.

4 12 Italian Me-109s come up to challenge the bombers.

5 Three of the fighters break off from the main formation, and prepare to attack the B-25s from the rear.

6 The main group of nine fighters feign an attack on the lead box of bombers, but do not engage

7 The three attacking Me-109s make a pass at the last box of bombers. Two come from 6 o'clock low, and one from 6 o'clock high. The high-fighter's guns hit two ships but do little damage; it passes right through the formation.

8 Joining up with the main fighter formation, the group attacks the last ships in an 18-ship B-25 formation heading toward another target in the Brenner Pass.

9 The bomber with the tail marking "60" is hit in the left engine, loses altitude, and speed and drops out of the formation.

10 Three fighters home in on the stricken aircraft, one accelerates forward, firing on the left engine causing the wing to detach and the aircraft to spiral to the ground.

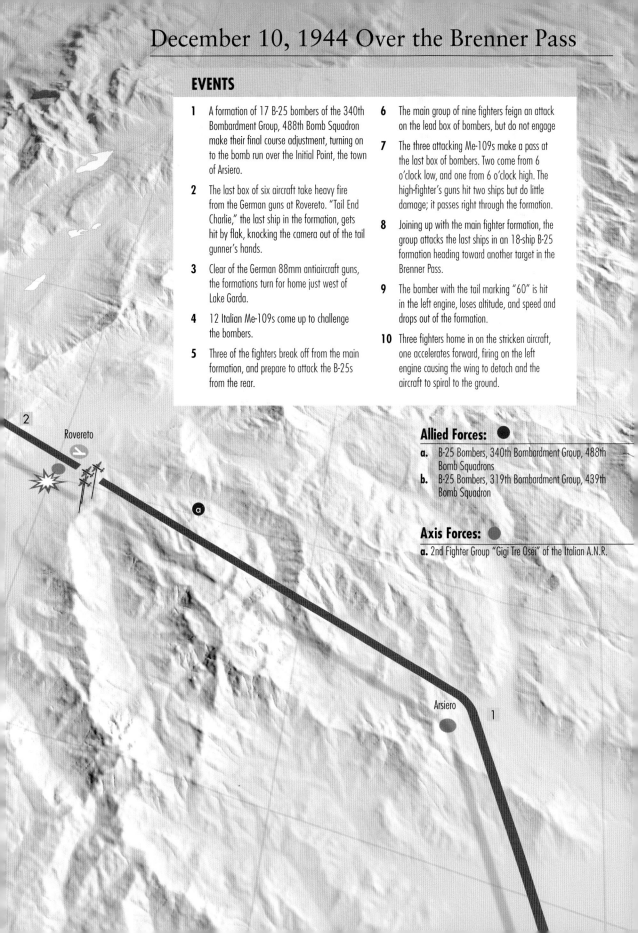

2

Rovereto

a

Allied Forces: ⬤
a. B-25 Bombers, 340th Bombardment Group, 488th Bomb Squadrons
b. B-25 Bombers, 319th Bombardment Group, 439th Bomb Squadron

Axis Forces: ⬤
a. 2nd Fighter Group "Gigi Tre Oséi" of the Italian A.N.R.

Arsiero

1

Planning the next mission. Note the circles on the map indicating the effective range of flak batteries along the route to the target. (57th Bomb Wing Archives, Anthony Hunter Collection)

successor to British Army General Sir Harold Alexander, in command of all Allied ground troops in Italy. More important was Clark's replacement: Lt General Lucian K. Truscott Jr's appointment as commanding general of Fifth Army was the most important assignment of senior leadership in the entire Italian campaign.

Truscott was the most successful American senior commander in the Mediterranean theater when it came to dealing effectively with the armed forces of other nations, a skill Mark Clark totally lacked. He was gruff, intent on getting things done efficiently, rather than a posing prima-donna like Patton or Clark. Truscott lacked the indecisiveness and incompetence that bedeviled so many of his contemporaries in North Africa and Italy, and he never, ever treated his soldiers or officers with the contempt for which Douglas MacArthur was so well-known. A more complete contrast to Clark could not be imagined.

Though Truscott had to suffer General Clark's repeated "show pony" performances, the morale of the whole Fifth Army benefited. Even on Corsica, Dan Bowling recalled that "things changed for the better after Christmas. There was a different attitude everywhere." Truscott was now in command of the most international of Allied forces. Fifth Army had more British, South African, Brazilian, Polish, and Italian troops than American. This had been a constant problem with Clark, whose decision that beating the British to Rome was more important than defeating the Wehrmacht in Italy had been the final straw for many of the foreign officers who served under him.

The hard winter of 1945

In January 1945, the three groups flew 48 missions and some 1,250 sorties. While adverse target weather kept the Mitchells on the ground on January 1 and 2, the bombers struck the lower Brenner bridges at Rovereto and Caliano over the next two days, with the weather then closing in from January 5–15. A report from the partisans stated that there had been no traffic on the Brenner line in either direction from January 1–7. Another source said that road traffic near Lake Garda had increased during this time, with 750 vehicles counted

The US Army was surprisingly tolerant of pilots "hot dogging" their aircraft. Here, pilots of the 321st Bomb Group treat the boys of the 340th Bomb Group to a "buzz" job. Note how some of the men involuntarily duck as the bombers come roaring in just above tree-top level. (57th Bomb Wing Archives, photo by Lt Glenn Pierre)

heading south and 940 heading north during the week. Thirty-nine missions over the month drew flak, with 224 aircraft hit and damaged, and five lost. Even in the face of this opposition, the bombers closed the pass to through traffic on five separate days; the Brenner was open for 12 days, from the 6th to the 15th and the 25th to the 27th of the month. On January 17 and 18, the bombers hit Ora and San Michele, and the bridge at Ala was destroyed before the weather closed in again on January 19.

Partisans reported that the line was only open to first-priority military traffic over the final week of the month, and that only three trains carrying ammunition and gasoline went south on the line. Moderate road traffic was noted during the days of bad weather, but the enemy was only able to use motor transport by diverting other urgently needed supplies from the trains to bring what gasoline made it to the lower Brenner. The flak was recorded as "hot and heavy" on all missions flown. The 340th Group's war diarist recorded that "milk runs [uneventful missions] are getting few and far between in northern Italy."

Yankee Doodle Dandy

Operation *Glass Knob* was the code name of the February 13, 1945, mission to San Ambrogio. A colonel had come up with the idea of bombing the rocky outcrop of the mountain next to the main road in order to cause a landslide which would block the road. The colonel flew on the mission as an observer in the lead ship.

Twelve aircraft of the 486th Squadron were loaded with 1,000lb bombs. Normally, after "Bombs Away," someone would yell, "Let's get the hell out of here!" and the formation would return to evasive action. But the colonel wanted to see the results of his plan, so the formation made a slow turn so that he could look back on his handiwork.

6Y, "Yankee Doodle Dandy," was in the No 6 position off the right wing of 6A, "Sahara Sue II." 6Y shuddered as it took a direct hit in the left engine. Pilot 1st Lieutenant Roman Figler told his co-pilot, 2nd Lieutenant James O'Connor, to feather the prop. The grim reply was, "I can't, the engine's gone!"

Figler headed the aircraft toward home, but near Rovereto they were hit by another burst of flak on the right side which took out the hydraulics, causing the wheels and flaps to drop and the bomb bay doors to fall open.

With the extra drag, 6Y could not maintain altitude and was facing mountains higher than they could climb. The order was given to bail out. The crew was taken prisoner immediately upon landing.

6W, flying in the same box of six aircraft, was also hit and unable to return to base.

The mountain resisted the onslaught of bombs; the road remained open.

The weather was such that there were several days of "severe clear" over Corsica where no missions could be flown due to heavy storms in the Alps. Such days were given over to training missions. On January 10, the 340th's Captain Saleem Aswad led five Mitchells for formation flight training. As they completed the flight, Aswad noticed the formation had grown by one, a B-25 carrying the markings of the 321st Group. With the 321st's Solenzara Field in sight not far away, Aswad gave a momentary thought to doing a low-level formation "buzz job," to see what the stranger might do. As he turned toward the field and prepared for the run, something told him it was a bad idea and he turned away with the rest of the formation following. As they passed over Solenzara at a proper altitude, the stranger peeled off and entered the landing pattern. On his return to Alesani, Aswad discovered just how lucky he had been. The B-25 that had joined up was being flown by 57th Wing commander Brigadier General Knapp himself, with the commanding officer of the 321st Group in the seat next to him!

The Russian winter offensive, which began on January 12, resulted in the Germans attempting to withdraw four divisions from the Gothic Line to the Eastern Front. The 356.Infanterie-Division began its withdrawal from Italy on January 15, but by the end of the month half the unit was still in Italy, unable to move due to the cuts made in the Brenner line. Units sat in trains on sidelines for days, waiting for repairs to be made. During that time, they were subject to strafing attacks from fighter-bombers that roamed the railway. With the bombers returning from January 28–31, the German division remained strung out and unavailable for use on either front.

The Brenner battle turned in the Allies' favor in February. The weather was so good throughout the month that there were only eight days when missions were not flown. As a result, the line was continuously blocked, which prevented the enemy building up any additional supplies and forced them to exist on what had been delivered earlier. By February 8, there were blocks at Lavis, where both the original viaduct and the diversion were unusable; Rovereto, where the bridge was heavily damaged; and Calliano, where the approaches to the bridge were badly cratered. With unfavorable weather from February 7–9, the German repair crews were able to open Calliano on February 10 and Rovereto the next day, but on February 10 the repaired bridge at Ala was destroyed, which blocked the line again until February 18. The bridge at Ala was attacked on 11 occasions by B-25s and five times by dive-bombing P-47s over the course of the month. Even with the repairs that were completed on February 18, the line was so badly blocked that southbound trains were forced to stop and unload their cargo into trucks for transport to the next open stretch of rail at three places; one trip from Munich to Bologna that had taken eight hours at the end of October – along with between eight and 12 others that day – now took five days in February, and the total delivered on each trip was less than half of what had been delivered per trip before Operation *Bingo* began.

The German command had begun moving the 16th SS Panzergrenadier Division out of the Gothic Line at the beginning of the month. Extracting the unit from Italy took three weeks and most of it was moved by motor transport, which burned up more of the enemy's precious gasoline supply.

In February 1945, the 310th Bomb Group flew a SHORAN mission to the Spilimbergo ammunition dump in northeast Italy, dropping through 10/10 undercast. The bombers felt the concussion from the explosions below, then saw columns of smoke break through the clouds, hinting at their success. (57th Bomb Wing Archives)

One-third of the division was held up at Adige due to lack of fuel for further movement, and there were reports of another unit attempting to buy fuel on the black market. Partisan sources reported that repairs on the line had been slowed because the repair units were taxed to their maximum to work on the increased damage.

During February, the bombers struck as far north as Innsbruck. Fortunately, even in Austria, the Luftwaffe was now so depleted there was no fighter opposition. The Germans shifted gun batteries north, increasing their number at Trento and Bressanone, while new batteries appeared at Lavis. The number of guns in the Brenner Pass rose to 482. It was a rare mission now that did not draw flak. The flak map Paul Young's bombardier used, with flak positions shown as red dots, had a solid red line half an inch wide, running from Verona to Innsbruck. "It seemed the guns were everywhere," Young remembered. Crews of the 340th Group, who had their worst month in terms of losses in February, described the flak as "murderous." Over the course of the month, six Mitchells were shot down, with 37 aircrew listed as missing in action and 11 others wounded in the bombers that made it back to Corsica.

At the end of February, the B-17s and B-24s of the XV Air Force hit the upper Brenner hard. The Bressanone bridge was rendered impassable, with both approaches badly cratered. Two spans of the Verona–Parona bridge were destroyed and the northern abutment severely damaged. The marshalling yards at Ora, Bolzano, Bressanone, Fortessa, Vipiteno, and Colle Isarco were also badly hit, with much rolling stock destroyed. After this, the only line south was the old standard-gauge single-track bypass line out of Verona. The end of February saw the line badly cut at nine different locations, interdicting the line throughout its length from Bolzano to Innsbruck.

Despite all this, the German early-warning system had been refined and the defenses increased. When an incoming formation got within 200km of a defended area, the gun batteries were alerted. When the formation reached within 80km, the guns were manned, with course and altitude given by the mountaintop observers. There were no surprise attacks.

The three groups flew 82 missions, with 1,771 sorties, during February. Sixty-two missions drew flak. Fourteen aircraft were lost and 305 were damaged, despite the introduction of white phosphorus for antiflak operations. With replacements few and far between as the higher US Army leadership looked to a final defeat of the Nazis in Germany itself, the mission total was changed again at the end of February, when the men were informed their tour was now "for the duration." Some tried to turn in their wings, willing to accept transfer to the infantry as an escape from the repeated missions into the Brenner Pass, but were refused. Paul Young recalled: "It really was like what was in the novel: you had to be crazy to continue, but if you tried to get out that meant you were sane and you had to stay. It wasn't called Catch-22 or anything, but the policy was there."

The defenses are strengthened

In March 1945, the number of flak batteries increased yet again, especially in the northern Brenner Pass. Forty-three new guns were added, for a total of 525. Ninety-six missions were flown during the month. Fifty-eight missions met flak, with 14 B-25s shot down and 207 suffering damage. The weather was so good this month that the bombers were able to strike on 24 of the 31 days. A new record was set for bridge destruction, with 41 of them knocked out, while 11 others were seriously damaged. The middle Brenner stretch was out of service the entire month, while the lower reaches were blocked for 29 days and the upper for 23 days. There was no through traffic, and a shipment from Munich to Bologna now had to be offloaded to trucks, reloaded on trains, then offloaded a total of 13 times along the route, and took eight days to make it through the pass. The 13 cuts were well-spaced through the 168-mile length of the line, doubling the manpower needed to shift the loads back and forth between trains and trucks.

The 715th Infantry Division was withdrawn from the Gothic Line at the end of February. By the end of March, only a third of the unit had managed to get to the Eastern Front. The three divisions that had been needed and might have made a difference in January only made their presence felt in mid-March, and then not at full-strength. At the same time, the German line in Italy had been weakened by the loss of the three divisions, just before the weather would change and allow the Allies to resume their offensive. Coal supplies for the line and Italian industries still operating had been barely met by shipments that came through Switzerland; however, on March 1, the Swiss government closed its borders, cutting off this supply line. By the middle of the month, it was reported that only 20 percent of needed minimum supplies were making it through. Between March 6 and 26, the skies were clear every day and missions were flown against every point of blockage to knock down repairs. The German repair crews were so overwhelmed by the damage that repairs which before had been made within 48 hours now took a week or more, and then only lasted a matter of days before they were damaged again.

The German experience

From January 30 until March 26, 1945, the Brenner line was cut somewhere every single day. Nevertheless, the fact that the line was out did not mean that no traffic was going through. It became necessary for the Germans to run separate trains through different sectors, which necessitated they unload and reload supplies, with consequent delay in delivery. By March, the trip from Munich to Bologna was still taking four to five days.

When not getting shot at by the Germans, Jerry Rosenthal liked to go skiing in the mountains of Corsica. He would complete 57 missions as a radioman-gunner. (57th Bomb Wing Archives)

In late February 1945, Oberfeldwebel Werner Mork returned to northern Italy from Germany after having been badly wounded during the fighting on the Gothic Line in October and evacuated to Germany. Writing after the war, he recalled his trip: "Once we got to the Brenner in Northern Italy, it was the train itself that suddenly became the target. From this point on there were many disrupted stretches of track and in particular damaged bridges. At those points we had to exit the train and make our way across the rickety rail bridges by foot to where another train waited on the other side. The Brenner train was no longer a reliable means of transportation; I frequently had to get out and walk. Sometimes, on the other side of a damaged bridge there wouldn't even be a train, but rather a line of trucks that would take us to the next rail station that was still intact. It had taken us a week to get from Trento to Mantua, a distance of 97 kilometers. All this sure raised our confidence that we would win the war."

Air combat with the ANR

The Italian ANR squadrons were seldom able to intercept the bombers, but there were three missions of note where the enemy fighters made an appearance.

The mission to bomb the bridge at Rovereto on December 10, 1944, was Jerry Rosenthal's first mission and he remembered it well. The 340th Group sent 36 planes from the four squadrons to hit the most deadly target in northern Italy. As he related: "There was no guessing about what the Rovereto flak gunners could do."

In the pre-mission briefing at 0800hrs, the crews were informed there was a possibility of enemy air activity, and that ten P-47s from the 57th Fighter Group were assigned as escort.

Rosenthal's plane for the mission was "8K," 43-27916, assigned as number four in the third six-plane box. After taking off at 0900hrs, the 18 B-25s from the 488th Squadron crossed into Italy just north of La Spezia and the crews donned their flak vests while the P-47s joined up and took position.

The bombers arrived at their Initial Point some 40 minutes later. Rosenthal remembered: "We were at 12,000[ft] over Lake Garda and climbed to 13,400 on the bomb run. No oxygen. I picked up the K-20 camera to get photos of our bombs away and maybe the bomb explosions of the leading boxes. The first box caught heavy, intense, and inaccurate flak at the beginning of the bomb run and we got heavy, intense, and accurate flak just before bombs away. My camera got jerked out of my hands when a flak burst came up through the floor [and] it got hit by shrapnel."

After releasing their bombs, the bombers broke their close formation. Rosenthal spotted six Bf-109s when they feinted an attack toward the lead squadron from 9 o'clock level, while three others attacked his formation, two from 6 o'clock left low and one from 6 o'clock right high.

Other enemy fighters hit a B-25 that exploded and another that spun in with both engines on fire. One enemy fighter flew through the formation; Rosenthal saw it coming but wasn't able to track it. Gunners in the formation managed to get one, while the P-47s knocked down four.

Rosenthal and the other 488th Bomb Squadron crewmen could finally catch their breath and take a look at what was going on around them. In the distance over Lake Garda, they saw the formation of Bf-109s which had harassed them, now attacking the B-25s from the 319th Bombardment Group. They watched in horror as one bomber was attacked multiple times, caught fire, lost a wing, and spiraled to the ground. Another bomber was seen to have an engine on fire.

The enemy fighters that attacked Rosenthal's formation had continued on and turned north to pursue another formation of B-25s. That formation of 18 B-25s belonged to the 319th Bombardment Group's 439th Bomb Squadron, tasked with bombing the rail bridge at San Michele all'Adige. The Flight Commander was Major R. K. Ketterer, and Flight Leader was 1st Lieutenant F. L. Green. Their assigned flight path had them flying to the west of Lake Garda parallel to the lake. Over the little town of Tione di Trento, they turned to a heading of 015 degrees for the bomb run. Just a few minutes before arrival over the target, they were jumped by the Bf-109s.

Flying in the number four position of the third box was B-25J "60" from the 439th Bomb Squadron, piloted by 1st Lieutenant Herbert Herman, with 2nd Lieutenant Royce E. Stephens as copilot. The rest of the crew were bombardier 1st Lieutenant Harold E. Smith,

Mission Report for the December 10, 1944, attack on Rovereto. The IP (Initial Point), the town of Arsiero, was the start of the bomb run. They had to fly straight and steady into the flak, with no evasive maneuvers until "bombs away." Flak was heavy-caliber, intense, and accurate. The Observations section describes the attack by the Italian Me-109s. (57th Bomb Wing Archives)

The ill-fated aircraft No 60, center, lower echelon, in flight. No 60 would be lost to Italian fighters over the Brenner Pass on December 10, 1944. (57th Bomb Wing Archives)

engineer-gunner Sergeant Joseph Pizzoferrato, radioman-gunner Sergeant George J. Stodghill, and tail gunner Sergeant Jasper F. Gosney.

Number 60 took a direct hit in the left engine, setting it on fire. Other aircraft in the formation called Lt Herman and told him that his engine was on fire; Herman dropped out of the formation since he had a full load of four 1,000lb bombs and could not risk having them explode and take out the other aircraft in the formation.

The single remaining engine was having trouble keeping the fully loaded aircraft aloft. Herman was losing altitude quickly, but kept the bomber under control. His real problem, however, was the three Bf-109s coming up on his rear. One fighter accelerated ahead of the others and made a firing pass. His rounds struck home and the left outer wing of the damaged Number 60 fell away.

On board the stricken aircraft, events moved quickly. Herman was heard to say multiple times, "I can't hold it much longer, I can't hold it much longer," then he gave the order for the crew to bail out. Stodghill and Gosney went out of the rear hatch. Co-pilot Stephens motioned Pizzoferrato and Smith to go out through the front hatch just behind the cockpit.

Smith reported that both rudders were shot off, and with the wing missing, the ship was spinning. He was lucky to be thrown clear of the out-of-control bomber as it spiraled down. When he last saw the pilots, Herman appeared to be injured, but Stephens was not. The two were doing everything they could to make sure their crew could escape. They did not. It was Lt Herman's 37th mission.

Pizzoferrato broke his ankle upon landing, and was captured straight away. The other three eluded immediate capture, but their luck ran out the next day and all three were taken into custody. The four spent the rest of the war as POWs, but returned home after liberation.

B-25 Number 60 went down in flames 2½ miles east of Marone in Lombardy. The 319th Bomb Group claimed five enemy fighters brought down during the mission, and one probable.

Sixty-four 1,000lb bombs were dropped in a good pattern on the bridge. The Rovereto gunners damaged ten Mitchells and wounded one crewman.

The third major air battle happened on March 23, 1945, and involved the 310th Group, which, having fought off the Luftwaffe over North Africa and Sicily, suffered their last loss due to enemy air action. Tasked with bombing the Pordenone railroad bridge, the formation was attacked by an estimated 20 ANR Bf-109s just as they broke from their bomb drop. Five of the fighters went after the B-25 flown by 2nd Lieutenant James J. Summers of the 380th Squadron, the trailing aircraft of the second box of six. Cannon fire struck the left engine and wing, and white smoke began to trail as the oil system was knocked out. The hydraulic system was also hit and the landing gear dropped down. With the extra drag, the bomber couldn't keep up with the others and dropped out of formation to the left. Inside, Summers and co-pilot 1st Lieutenant Alex Zebelian Jr fought to maintain control as the Mitchell headed toward the mountains below. The tail gunner and radioman went out of the rear hatch, while the bombardier kicked open the forward hatch and threw himself out. Their parachutes blossomed quickly. Several enemy fighters pressed a second attack and set the damaged engine on fire, which quickly spread to the wing. The Spitfire escort then finally arrived and drove the enemy fighters off as the pilot, co-pilot, and turret gunner made their exit. By the end of the month, the co-pilot, turret gunner, and bombardier were back on Corsica, having been rescued by partisans. The others had been captured and made prisoner.

Captain Everett Robinson flew the lead plane of the formation from the 380th Squadron. The second attack by the Italian fighters hit his B-25 in the engine before being driven off by the escorts. Robinson managed to hold the badly damaged bomber in the air to return to Ghisonaccia on Corsica, where he made a successful emergency landing; he was awarded a Distinguished Flying Cross for bringing his crew home uninjured.

The last formation attacked were the 12 B-25s from the 379th Squadron. Flying lead for the third box of six was 1st Lieutenant John M. Ford, with his co-pilot 1st Lieutenant William Poole. Two Bf-109s hit the bomber in its right engine, which caught fire. Ford held formation until his bombardier could drop on the bridge before diving to put out the flames, then brought the bomber safely home.

The top turret gunner in wingman 1st Lieutenant Walter E. Grauman's B-25 opened fire as the Bf-109s flashed past, and one was seen to be smoking as it turned away. Altogether, the bombers and their escort accounted for four enemy fighters shot down and three damaged.

The campaign crescendos

On March 10, the crew of "Puss 'n Boots," a B-25 that arrived on Corsica the previous May, flew their last mission, perhaps the toughest the 310th Group flew in the Brenner Pass campaign.

The main rail line ran through the town of Ora. A nearby bridge that had been previously knocked out had been repaired so that a single track was operational. A new line had also been constructed around a previously bombed area and was also now usable. Two missions were planned to hit both targets. Forty-eight B-25s from the 379th, 380th, 381st, and 428th Squadrons of the 310th would each carry four 1,000lb bombs. Seven more would carry 100lb white phosphorus bombs and 20lb fragmentation bombs. Six others would fly as antiflak suppression, while one

"Puss 'n Boots" with two unidentified airmen. On the March 10, 1945, mission to Ora, this bomber was hit multiple times by intense flak. The pilot managed to nurse it back to the base on Corsica, but it had to be abandoned before landing. (57th Bomb Wing Archives)

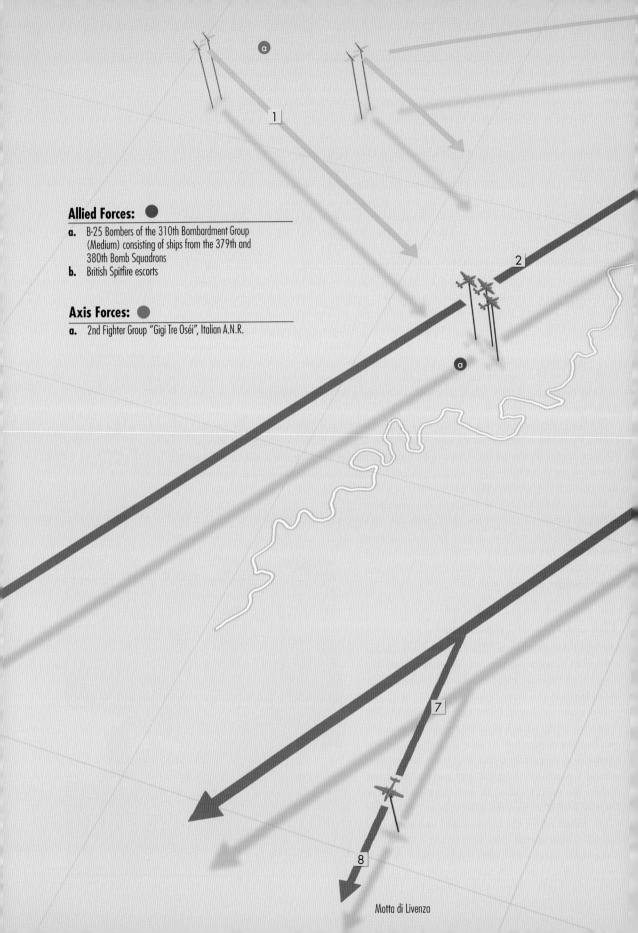

Allied Forces: ●

a. B-25 Bombers of the 310th Bombardment Group (Medium) consisting of ships from the 379th and 380th Bomb Squadrons

b. British Spitfire escorts

Axis Forces: ●

a. 2nd Fighter Group "Gigi Tre Oséi", Italian A.N.R.

Motta di Livenza

Air Battle over Pordenone March 23, 1945

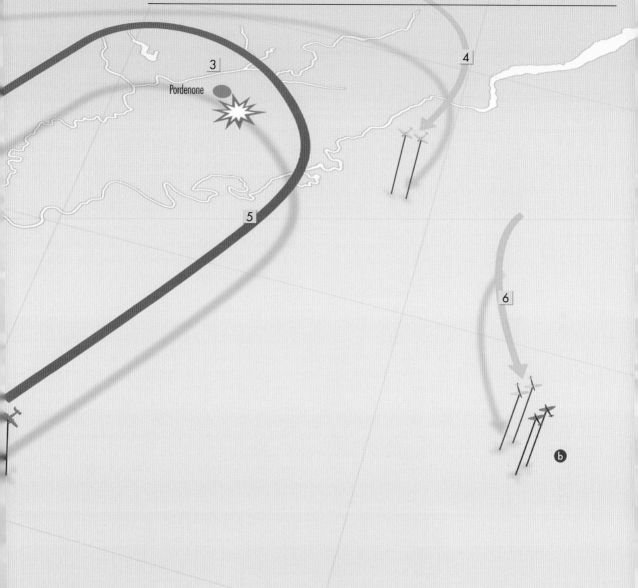

Pordenone

EVENTS

1 Fifteen to twenty Me-109 fighters of the Italian A.N.R. come out of the sun to attack the first and second elements of the B-25 bomber formation.

2 The fighters inflict major damage on two aircraft.

3 The pilots of the two stricken bombers manage to keep their aircraft under control and complete the bombing run on the railroad bridge at Pordenone. The fighters break off their attack while the bombers are over the target to avoid any antiaircraft fire.

4 The fighters renew their attack immediately after the bombers turn off the bombing run.

5 The ship "Sitting Pretty" is hit in the left engine.

6 The British Spitfires acting as escorts for the bombers finally materialize and join the fight, engaging several of the Me-109s in a dogfight.

7 The remaining Me-109s continue the attack hitting "Sitting Pretty" again in the left engine, setting it on fire.

8 Crewmen bail out and the pilots try to keep "Sitting Pretty" on a stable glide, hoping to make it to the sea. It was last observed by the rest of the formation descending to 4,000 then 2,000ft, then crashing near Motta di Livenza.

antiflak and six regular spares would follow the formation. The Group Operations Officer, Major Royal Allison, and 379th Squadron Operations Officer, Major Carl E. Rice, decided to lead the two flights themselves.

The plan of attack was for the six antiflak bombers from the 381st Squadron to precede the main formation and hit the gun positions. Thirty-two enemy guns were reported clustered in the area, both German 88s and Italian 105s. Twenty-four main force bombers from the 379th and 380th Squadrons would bomb the railroad bridge, while 18 B-25s from the 428th Squadron would bomb the diversion line.

The bombers crossed the Italian coast north of La Spezia and climbed to cross the snowy peaks. Ahead of the main formation, the six antiflak ships ran into heavy defensive fire before they had a chance to drop their bombs. The Germans lit smoke pots that obscured the targets. Box after box of the B-25s flew into the worst flak the crews had ever seen. Three bombers were shot down on the bomb run, while a fourth crashed after dropping its bombs and attempting to turn away, with ten more crippled from flak hits. Major Allison reported: "The flak was everywhere – intense, heavy, and accurate. Going into it seemed like a suicidal act. The first box was badly shot up and their plight could be seen by the others. The succeeding boxes went right in regardless." Major Rice remembered: "Never have I heard so many flak bursts as on the bomb run that day."

"Puss 'n Boots," flown by 1st Lieutenant George F. Tilley Jr, was in the first box. The B-25 was severely damaged and forced out of formation. Bombardier 2nd Lieutenant Russell Grigsby recalled: "We had broken away from the main formation a few minutes away from the IP, when wham-wham-wham-wham, four bursts of flak exploded right below us." The flak riddled "Puss 'n Boots" and tore gaping holes in the wings, both engine nacelles, the cockpit – where large fragments smashed all but three instruments – and the radioman's station. The main hydraulic lines were completely severed and the emergency system was shot away. The landing gear and flaps were now inoperable. "The right engine was smoking," Grigsby later wrote, "and several gas lines had been cut so that fuel began to pour into the turret gunner's and radioman's compartments."

Miraculously, none of the crew had been hit, though daylight poured through the fuselage. Tilley feathered the right engine, which extinguished the flames. With the bomber going

Captain Royal Allison at the officers' club of the 310th Bomb Group in Tunisia. Later promoted to major, he served as Group Operations Officer for the 310th and flew on the disastrous March 10 mission to Ora. (57th Bomb Wing Archives)

down, the choice was bailing out over the target or attempting to restart the engine with the chance it might explode. After several failed attempts, Tilley managed to get the engine running again. Realizing he had no airspeed indicator, Tilley called on the still-working radio for help. First Lieutenant Victor Irons brought his Mitchell alongside the wounded "Puss 'n Boots."

"Puss 'n Boots" hung together long enough to cross the Ligurian Sea to Corsica. Over the island, Grigsby and engineer-gunner Staff Sergeant George McTavey attempted to crank open the bomb doors to get rid of the bombs, but it was impossible. They then tried unsuccessfully to crank down the landing gear. "By this time the fuel was ankle deep in both forward and rear compartments, and with the fumes we had to fight nausea as well as broken controls and flames."

A second attempt was made to lower the wheels. When that failed, Tilley pulled up and told the crew to prepare to bail out. Grigsby went out of the lower forward hatch, followed by the navigator and co-pilot, while the radioman and tail gunner exited via the rear lower hatch. Tilley trimmed the bomber and headed it out to sea, then bailed out successfully. He was awarded the DFC for saving his crew. Lieutenant Irons, who had escorted "Puss 'n Boots" home despite heavy damage to his own plane, was also awarded the DFC.

Flak damage: note the fuselage is also riddled with holes. (57th Bomb Wing Archives)

The B-25 flown by 1st Lieutenant George Rorer, who had survived a mid-air collision the previous September, was badly hit and caught fire in the right engine nacelle. With his co-pilot too seriously injured to bail out, Rorer attempted a crash landing. As he touched down, the right wingtip caught a tree. The Mitchell cartwheeled, burst into flames, and broke in two. There were no survivors.

The 428th Squadron B-25 flown by 1st Lieutenant Jordan Keister was hit and the right engine and nacelle burst into flames as the bomber fell behind the formation. As Keister fought to control the stricken bomber, others saw four parachutes blossom when the crew bailed out. Moments later, the right wing tore off and the Mitchell spun in, exploding on impact.

Five pilots of the 379th Squadron – Lieutenants George Parry, Richard McEldery, Andrew Dennis, Noah T. Shirley, and Gordon M. Jacobs – were awarded the DFC for bringing their badly shot-up bombers back successfully to save their crews.

Amazingly, despite the deadly flak that badly damaged 18 of the 48 bombers and destroyed four others, there were few men wounded. Multiple holes in areas occupied by crewmen should have caused wounds, but didn't. Several returned with plexiglass hanging in pieces in the

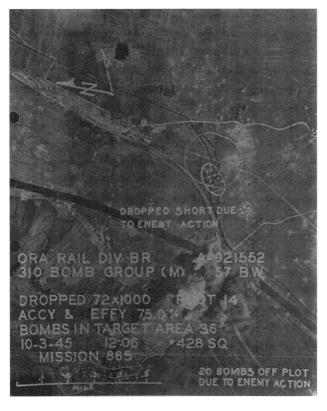

ORA RAIL DIV BR A 921552
310 BOMB GROUP (M) 57 B.W.

DROPPED 72x1000 FT T 14
ACCY & EFFY 75.0 %
BOMBS IN TARGET AREA 36
10-3-45 12:06 428 SQ
MISSION 865

DROPPED SHORT DUE
TO ENEMY ACTION

20 BOMBS OFF PLOT
DUE TO ENEMY ACTION

Results of the bombing raid on Ora on March 10, 1945. The Mission Report read: "Intense, heavy, accurate flak from target holed six aircraft. First aircraft crash-landed, wing torn off, burst into flames and broke apart, crew was unable to get out of plane. Second aircraft crashed and exploded, Six chutes seen to open. Third aircraft seen to be hit and right wing torn off. Last seen spinning in."(57th Bomb Wing Archives)

bombardiers' greenhouses, yet all escaped uninjured. Ruptured gas lines and fuel tanks sprayed gasoline into fuselages, but no one was burned.

Despite everything, the railroad was cut in several places and the bridge so badly damaged it could not be repaired before the end of the war. The 310th Bomb Group was awarded a second Distinguished Unit Citation for the Ora bridge mission.

Paul Young long remembered his 37th mission, flown on March 24, 1945: "As we flew away from the target, the guys in back called on the intercom to ask if we had taken a hit up front, since things were 'very windy back here.' We checked everywhere, but there was no damage. Our radioman then crawled into the space over the bomb bay and opened the inspection hatch, to discover that one of our thousand pounders had hung up by its tail shackles. It was hanging out the bomb bay, preventing the doors from closing. Not only that, but the arming propeller on the nose was spinning. I looked over at my co-pilot. Our first reaction was to bail out before the bomb was fully armed. But we were still 30 miles behind the lines, over enemy territory. There was a quick crew conference on the intercom and the radioman said he'd try something to get rid of the bomb first before we bailed out. He then shucked his gear and lowered himself through that small inspection hatch in the roof of the bomb bay to hang by his arms while he repeatedly kicked the bomb. After what seemed an eternity, the tail gunner reported the bomb had fallen free. He then pulled the radioman out of the bomb bay, which our bombardier was able to close. When we got back home, the first thing I did was write up a recommendation for a Distinguished Flying Cross for our radioman." The squadron's War Diary made no special mention of the event, noting only that three 1,000lb bombs were jettisoned after the mission: two at sea and one "over enemy territory."

The rains that came for the first time in two months at the end of March gave the crews of the 57th Bomb Wing a five-day respite from operations, which was considered a mixed blessing. While the crews got some much-needed rest, the Germans had five bomb-free days for their repair crews to work on a railroad system that had been made practically impassable.

On April 6, the Quartermaster General of the German Fourteenth Army reported that it took four to five days for a shipment of supplies to get through the Brenner Pass. During March, an average of 1,800 tons of supplies arrived each day, less than half the daily minimum necessary to sustain operations. The Allied offensive now awaited the spring thaw.

The final month

The war's final month saw the bombers of the 57th Wing leave Corsica in early April 1945 after being in residence for a year. As the front lines in northern Italy moved, Corsica was too distant to allow the Mitchells to operate with full bomb loads.

The 310th Group commenced their move from Ghisonaccia to Fano, on the Adriatic coast, on March 30. The move to Fano was accomplished over the first ten days of April, with the

The living conditions on Corsica for the 340th Bomb Group were primitive. The men were quartered in tents, and even the enlisted men's club, shown here, was a tent. (Hymie Setzer Collection)

main group arriving by April 6. The men were impressed to find Fano was a neat, well-built seaside town at the end of the old Roman Via Flaminia, that had largely escaped the ravages of war as the Allies advanced up the Adriatic coast, with the airfield a mile south of town. Line personnel were quartered in several long, single-story masonry structures that had been divided into three-room apartments, and there were hangar facilities for maintenance. The Mitchells shared the field with Royal Air Force and South African Air Force tactical squadrons, comprised of Spitfires, P-40 Kittyhawk dive-bombers, Beaufighters, Mosquitos, and B-26 Marauders flown by the South Africans.

It all changed when the 340th BG moved to Rimini. The officers' club could offer a live band, and there were girls to dance with. However, since the British and other Allies were in town, the men had to wear Class A jackets and ties. It was a big change from the relaxed atmosphere on Corsica. One GI complained: "It's like being back in the Army again." (57th Bomb Wing Archives)

Ground crew work on an engine in the open air on Corsica. Often the ground crews would pitch their tents near the hardstands where the aircraft they were maintaining would be parked. When the Germans bombed the airfield at Alesani, the majority of the casualties were ground crew bivouacked near the aircraft being targeted by the Luftwaffe. (57th Bomb Wing Archives, Charles Berman Collection)

The 340th Group began its move to Rimini, a former pre-war Regia Aeronautica base south of Venice on the Adriatic coast, on April 4. The men were happy to discover their quarters at the new base would be in Miramare and Riccione, towns which had been popular before the war as fashionable summer resorts. At last they would be living indoors. The group's war diarist noted: "The rooms have running water, are wired for lights, and have suffered no bomb or shell damage. Everybody is blinking with amazement at finding himself plunked down in this pleasant little town with fairly well-dressed people, attractive girls, and small shops."

On April 6, the group flew its last missions from Alesani. The B-25s attacked the Poggio Rusco rail bridge and a ship in La Spezia harbor, both of which were missed, and also targeted a coastal gun near La Spezia that was holding up the advance of the 92nd Division on the town of Massa, with good results. The Mitchells then flew on to the new field outside Rimini to take up permanent residence.

While the 340th Group moved to Rimini, the 321st had moved from Solenzara to Falconara a week earlier. On April 5, the 321st flew their first mission from the Italian mainland. While missions were still being flown into the Brenner Pass, the emphasis had changed to missions in direct support of the coming Allied ground offensive. Dan Bowling, now promoted to captain, led 20 445th Squadron bombers as part of an 80-plane strike against German Defense Area "Harry," with the bombers dropping fragmentation bombs against gun positions and troop emplacements.

Sergeant Bernard Seegmiller, the 445th Squadron's chief armorer, arrived at Falconara on April 7 and recorded his impressions in his diary two days later: "We arrived here the afternoon of the 7th by C-47. The weather was quite bad and we flew blind most of the way. Some of our B-25s were forced to turn back on account of icing conditions. We are quartered inside a huge compound which accommodates the entire group. Each squadron occupies a barracks that is complete with showers, kitchen, administration, and latrines. The construction is brick with tile floors and a great deal of marble. Some improvising has been done to convert the squat-down latrines into showers. I am told this place was built as a cavalry base by the Mussolini gang. It is very elaborate and well laid out. The field is very well laid out and steel planking covers the runway and taxi strips and hardstands. A British outfit built the landing facility and are still operating with Spits, Beaufighters, Mosquitos, and PBYs. Fifteenth Air Force heavies frequently land here on emergency returns from targets in Germany and Austria. Several have come in badly shot up since we came over."

The 321st Group's ground crews were most happy to find that there were large hangars at Falconara. Finally, difficult jobs like engine changes could be done inside, with proper equipment for removing and replacing engines and for performing other major repair of shot-up airplanes, all of which had been previously performed in the open on Corsica.

One thing the men of all three groups noticed quickly was the widespread presence of military police. Gone were the carefree days on Corsica of not worrying overmuch about a shave, whether clothes were oil-stained, and whether all officers were properly saluted by the men, and for the junior officers, whether their seniors were shown proper "military courtesy." As Dan Bowling's crew chief, Master Sergeant Fred Lawrence, put it in a letter home, "people are complaining about having rejoined the Army."

The final Allied offensive

The Allies' final offensive in Italy commenced on April 9, 1945, with massive aerial and artillery bombardments. At the end of the first day, Sergeant Seegmiller recorded his memories: "Today has been a big one. Every available aircraft in the theater operated in preparing a push-off for the Eighth and Fifth Armies. It began about 1500 hours and we watched every type of plane in the American Air Force go over like great flocks of geese as

The marshalling yard at Novara, located just west of Milan, was enormous and of exceptional importance to the rail system. On March 10, 1945, the 310th Bomb Group attacked the yards with devastating accuracy and effect. (57th Bomb Wing Archives, Edward Betts Collection)

General Heinrich von Vietinghoff, commander of the German Tenth Army, stated: "The crossings of the Reno and the Po were decisively influenced by the employment of the Allied Air Forces. The smashing of almost all ferries and bridges made an ordered retreat across the Po no longer possible. The troops amassed at the crossing points often had to swim to the other bank without heavy weapons." (ullstein bild via Getty Images)

our own were taking off. It was an impressive sight and I could not help thinking, 'Those poor damn Germans.'"

The 57th Wing flew a "maximum effort" in support of the Allied armies, with each group and each squadron flying multiple missions. The 340th Group's war diarist, 1st Lieutenant Glenn Pierre, wrote of the day: "A terrific air pounding of German positions northeast and east of Bologna by 600 bombers and hundreds of fighters starting shortly after one o'clock. 340th group put up 76 aircraft, almost half the B-25 wing effort. Our targets were two artillery concentration areas near Imola. Photo Interpreter says most of the 13 boxes of six aircraft each bombed very accurately. After the air attacks had ceased – about 1800 hours – the artillery got going and the Polish corps and the 10th British Corps, whom we were supporting, jumped off over the Senio river, bound for the banks of the Santerno river, the first pause point."

Two days later on April 11, 321st Group war diarist Captain Paul Jackson wrote: "With the new Italian offensive rolling along, the target for today was the Argenta Reserve Area. Wing called for another maximum-effort day and we came through with 48 Mitchells taking off at 0758 hours and 24 more taking off at 0853 hours. The past three days, briefings have begun in the early morning darkness; but no one seems to mind it, just so the offensive keeps going. The combined frag-load this morning was 8,520 fragmentation bombs and it forebodes another bad day for German GIs. The first formation over ran into heavy, moderate, accurate flak and one plane received a hit in the tail while on the bomb-run. It was last seen turning east and losing altitude rapidly. The second formation also ran into heavy flak and returned with three aircraft holed. The consolation was a 99 percent accuracy. After a hurried noon chow and darn little sack time, 24 planes went out for the San Ambrogio Rail Culvert at 1430 hours, and 18 more headed for the Volargne Rail Fill at 1540 hours."

Mission 846, to bomb the German troop assembly area at Argenta in front of the Australian Division of the Eighth Army, was Dan Bowling's 60th and most memorable mission of the war. He led 18 445th Squadron B-25s at the forefront of a formation from all four of the 321st Group's squadrons in B-25J "Flo," one of the newest aircraft in the squadron, with co-pilot 2nd Lieutenant Paul Riggenbach, navigator 1st Lieutenant Robert Mitchell guiding the formation to the target, and bombardier 1st Lieutenant Joe Silnutzer as group lead on whose aim all others would depend. Fourteen Mitchells from the 446th Squadron followed Bowling's formation, led by Major Robert Smedley in "Merrily We Bomb Along." Six B-25s of the 447th Squadron led by 1st Lieutenant Norman Rose in "Number 62" were right behind, while 1st Lieutenant W. F. Autrey in B-25J "Number 86" led ten 448th Squadron planes in the rear.

The pre-mission briefing emphasized that timing was of the essence. There were two German divisions at Argenta which it was feared were ready to attempt a counterattack. Bowling, Silnutzer, and Mitchell were told the Allied troops would light smoke pots to mark the lines, since the target was very close to the Allied positions. "If the white smoke changes to yellow, do not bomb," was the order. Yellow smoke would signify that the Allied troops had begun their attack. After the numerous occasions throughout the war when Allied bombers had hit their own side at places like Cassino in central Italy and St Lo in northern France, it was crucial for the bombers to arrive over the target on time, ahead of the attack.

The thousands of 20lb fragmentation bombs they would shower over the enemy formations would give the Allied troops the cover they needed at the moment they started their advance. At the last minute, Bowling asked for information on the defenses and was informed there were over 200 antiaircraft weapons. He recalled: "We were to bomb at 10,500ft and 200mph. This was the most heavily-defended target we had gone against. I knew it was going to be tough."

Takeoff was at 0758hrs. Both Silnutzer and Mitchell had argued with Bowling about taking a new airplane on its first mission. A foretaste of things to come this day was offered when the right engine took three attempts to get it to turn over properly and start. On the runway, there was a sharp drop on the right engine magnetos when Bowling checked them prior to takeoff. With one turn over the field for the aircraft to join up, he led the 48 Mitchells on the 40-minute flight north over the Adriatic to Ravenna, where they turned inland and headed for Argenta. "When we were climbing to 10,500ft, I realized the plane was very sluggish," Bowling recounted. "When we got to altitude, I had to set the engines at nearly full-throttle to maintain 200 miles an hour, and the cylinder head temperatures on both engines were nearly at the red line." This meant severe problems for Bowling, who was now eight minutes ahead of schedule for hitting the target.

The ground echelon was ordered to "Keep 'em Flying." For engineer personnel that meant ridding the machinery of gremlins that prevented the equipment from functioning properly. (57th Bomb Wing Archives)

"I had to do something to save the engines, so I notified the formation I was reducing speed [by] 20 miles an hour and climbing 500ft. Three minutes from the target, we would dive back down to the correct altitude and pick up the right speed." It was crucially important the formation had the right speed and altitude when they dropped their loads, since those were the settings in the Norden bombsights, and any variance would mean they could not make an accurate drop.

The bombers arrived over the target three minutes early and Bowling increased power as he dived back to 10,500ft and picked up speed back to 200mph. "Suddenly all hell broke loose with black flak puffs right where we would have been had I not dived and picked up speed. Those flak gunners were right on us. Joe opened the bomb bay." As the bombers turned onto their run, Mitchell called that he saw yellow smoke on the ground. Silnutzer replied "bomb doors closing." Bowling sensed something wrong and screamed at his bombardier to reopen the doors. "Roll forward six or seven hundred feet and bomb! I'll take the blame!"

Mitchell kept arguing they had to abort, that they were too late. "Then the flak was all around us. The plane on our right was hit twice and gone. I pulled to the right and had both engines past the red line, waiting for them to explode." The formation followed, using Bowling's tactic to evade as the German gunners put solid fields of exploding flak where they would have been. "They were ten seconds too late to get us." They turned back left and 45 seconds later Silnutzer announced "bombs away!".

The B-25 was very versatile in the types of bomb load it could carry. Here, aircraft of the 310th Bomb Group drop fragmentation bombs on enemy troop concentrations. (57th Bomb Wing Archives, Edward Betts Collection)

CLOSE SUPPORT

On a bomb run it was essential that the box of six aircraft maintain a tight formation to ensure that the bombs hit in a compact pattern on the pinpoint targets. This photo shows how close the bombers flew. Given the air turbulence over the Alps, it added yet another danger to the missions. (57th Bomb Wing Archives, Edward Betts Collection)

Bowling immediately rolled left and reduced power. "The engines sounded ready to blow, so I got us headed back to the Adriatic, where at least we'd have a chance of being picked up. Moments later, the cylinder head temperatures came back down to red line. Still dangerous, but now with the bomber in a dive for the coast, cooler air was circulating through the cowling."

Forty minutes later, they were back at Falconara. Bowling taxied to the hardstand, where two jeeps with four officers were waiting. "I thought we'd done it; hit our own troops." He shut down while Silnutzer and Mitchell climbed out. "I saw it was the intel officer, ops officer, group bombardier, and the deputy group CO. I figured we'd had it." And then the four were grabbing Silnutzer and Mitchell and shaking their hands. When Bowling crawled out, Colonel Young, the deputy group CO, told him the mission had been perfect, that they had hit the Germans directly on target with a 100 percent drop.

The next day, Line Chief Master Sergeant Mitchell told Bowling that the engines on "Flo" had not been reset after its arrival in the group. When planes were flown across the South Atlantic, the engine power settings were adjusted for long-range cruise power settings needed for the delivery flight. It had indeed been a very near thing that Bowling had not lost both engines in his attack run.

The success at Argenta was marred by the loss of "Maggie," the B-25 flown by 1st Lieutenant Lewis Dentoni that had been hit and forced out of formation from Bowling's right wing as they entered the bomb run. Flak hit the tail and shattered it; everyone who saw the hit believed it likely killed tail gunner Staff Sergeant David Morisi immediately, since they had seen him blown out of the tail. Other crews reported seeing the bomber at 6,000ft over Lake Comacchio as it tipped over into a spin. One gunner thought he saw two parachutes pop open before the bomber crashed just behind Allied lines and caught fire, but no one was ever found. First Lieutenant Max Lewis, normally a first pilot, had flown the mission when his tentmate, Dentoni's co-pilot, reported an ear infection. Silnutzer was hit hard by the loss; he had shared his tent with Dentoni and Lewis since he arrived on Corsica, and the three were close friends who had gone to Rome and Capri together on leaves. Tail gunner Morisi had flown several missions with Bowling.

Amazingly, Morisi had survived; the impact of the hit had knocked him unconscious and blown him out of the airplane still in his seat with all equipment still attached. He came to and unhooked his seatbelt so his seat and armor plate fell to the ground below. The young sergeant pulled his ripcord and came down just north of the battle line, where he was captured by the Germans and spent the final weeks of the war as a prisoner.

The next day, the group was informed that the officer in charge of setting the smoke pots on the ground had mistakenly fired the flare that meant the yellow smoke pots were to be lit, rather than the correct white pots. The troops reported that the Germans were in shock from the bombing when they went over to the attack. Several thousand were killed and wounded, and the Australians took over 3,500 prisoners.

Bad weather soon returned, and the 321st Group stood down following a mission to Yugoslavia on April 12. Sergeant Seegmiller discovered that there was a downside to living inside a barracks, which he recorded in his diary: "It's cold and noisy in these brick barracks. Today I asked Captain Johnson if something couldn't be done for us armorers so we could get some sleep at night. He arranged to move us all to a single bay in the far end and partition it off from the rest which was quite decent of him. The first several days after we got here

Aircrews treasured the resilience of the B-25. In this photo we see part of the nose assembly shot off by flak during a sea sweep on February 23, 1943. Note the flak holes in the side of the aircraft and the bent propeller. In spite of the damage, the pilot was able to bring the B-25 and its crew home safely. (57th Bomb Wing Archives, Edward Betts Collection)

On April 16, 1945, elements of the 340th Bomb Group went after a railroad bridge over the Reno River just northwest of Bologna. The weather was poor and the first flight returned without dropping. The second flight had a failure of "special equipment," meaning SHORAN. Undeterred, on the 17th they returned to do a proper job on the bridge. (57th Bomb Wing Archives, Edward Betts Collection)

we worked almost constantly and all of us were completely worn out. Things have sort of slacked off since then. Yesterday a bomb fell on Bob Long and injured his back and foot. He was taken to the hospital and the report we have so far says he has a fractured spine and will be in a cast several months."

On the morning of Friday, April 13, the men in the three groups learned of the death of President Franklin D. Roosevelt as they stood in line for breakfast. For many, he was the only president they could remember.

On Saturday, April 14, the US Fifth Army offensive toward Bologna began. The attack was preceded by a 30-minute wave of bombing from B-25s dropping fragmentation bombs and

Also on the 17th of April the 321st Bomb Group made an attack on an important road bridge over the Reno River on Highway 9 running parallel to the Rimini-Piacenza rail line. Destruction of this bridge made necessary a 14-mile detour through Caselecchio. (57th Bomb Wing Archives, Edward Betts Collection)

On April 5, 1945, the 310th Bomb Group attacked the rail bridge north of Modena. The bridge was an important link between Verona and Modena which joined the Bologna–Milan system. A direct hit on one of the piers destroyed the center span, which fell into the river bed. The enemy abandoned all repair efforts. (57th Bomb Wing Archives, Edward Betts Collection)

P-47s rocketing and strafing the German positions, following a 30-minute artillery barrage. Sergeant Hugh Evans of Item Company, 85th Mountain Infantry Regiment, 10th Mountain Division, remembered: "I had never seen anything like that, seen so many airplanes. You couldn't believe anyone could survive that."

The Morning Report of the 86th Infantry recorded: "Promptly at 0830 the airplanes began to circle lazily over the front lines, to be greeted with shouts and waves from the troops below. The planes moved over the valley and let loose with firebombs over Rocca di Roffeno. Great geysers of flame and heavy black smoke rose up to 200ft in the air, and the concussion could be felt 3,000 yards away. When the planes had finished, the artillery opened up, seemingly pounding every spot that the Air Corps had missed. In a few moments the valley was almost completely obscured by a fog of gray, black, and white smoke. The bursting shells started rock slides on the shale slopes of Rocca di Roffeno, and buildings were reduced to irregular piles of rubble."

Unfortunately, the barrage and bombing were not as effective as had been the case at Argenta, due to hazy weather that prevented fully accurate bombing. When the 85th and 87th regiments attacked Hills 903 and 913 near Castel d'Aiano, the fighting was fierce and 553 men were killed, wounded, or missing that first day. Among the wounded was a 21-year-old from Kansas, platoon leader 2nd Lieutenant Robert J. Dole of Item Company, who was badly injured by machine-gun fire that hit his upper back and right arm. When fellow soldiers saw how bad his injuries were, all they could do was give him the largest dose of morphine they dared and write an "M" for "morphine" on his forehead with his own blood, so that no one who found him would give him a second, fatal dose. They then had to leave him behind as they continued the advance.

While the 10th Mountain Division fought at Castel d'Aiano, the first two flights of the 445th Squadron successfully attacked Argenta again, using SHORAN to bomb through the clouds, though the third flight did not drop due to malfunction of the SHORAN gear. That afternoon, Dan Bowling was rolling down the runway to take off for another mission to hit German artillery outside Bologna when he was surprised to see a Bf-109 flash past as

In mid-April 1945, the pilot of this Croatian Me-109 decided that the war was over for him. He nearly collided with Dan Bowling's aircraft while landing at the 321st Bomb Group airfield at Fano in Italy. (57th Bomb Wing Archives)

the pilot dropped his landing gear and put the fighter down on the runway, barely missing Bowling, who managed to get airborne despite the near collision. When he turned over the field and looked down, Bowling could see the enemy fighter parked beside the runway, with the pilot out of the cockpit surrounded by ground personnel. "It turned out he was in the Croatian Air Force fighting for the Germans, and had decided today was a good day to end his war, so he flew over from Yugoslavia and landed at the first field he found, which happened to be ours."

With the Brenner rail line completely disrupted by the six-month bombing campaign, the end came quickly along the Gothic Line. On April 18, Eighth Army units in the east broke through the Argenta Gap and sent armor forward to encircle the German Tenth Army and meet the American IV Corps which advanced from central Italy. The remaining defenders of Bologna were trapped.

Dan Bowling flew what would turn out to be his final mission of the war on April 19. The target was the Vignola road bridge between Bologna and Modena, which separated the headquarters of the 90th Panzergrenadier Division from the unit's vehicle storage park. Bowling led six bombers from the 445th Squadron, with seven from the 446th following. It wasn't possible to put together the usual 18-plane formation since flight operations that day were so heavy. Despite getting heavy flak from two six-gun 88mm batteries, the two formations hit the target with extremely close bomb patterns over the entire 300ft bridge, with four spans destroyed and one seriously damaged. The mission went into the 321st Group's record book as "Mission of the Month." When he returned to Falconara, Bowling learned he was being taken off flying duties. Offered a promotion to major if he remained with the unit, he declined the honor and took the orders that arrived two weeks later sending him home.

Bologna fell on April 21, when the Polish 3rd Carpathian Division and the Italian Friuli Group from Eighth Army, and the US 34th Infantry Division from Fifth Army, entered the city. Bypassing Bologna, the 10th Mountain Division reached the Po River the next day and the Eighth Army's 8th Indian Infantry Division joined them a day later. The 340th Group's war diarist wrote: "Bologna has fallen to the Fifth and Eighth armies, it was announced today. Air support undoubtedly was a big key in making the Germans release their iron grip of last autumn and winter. With their supplies cut off by bombing and communications badly slashed, the Germans could only fall back under the tremendous armored drive of our Allied 15th Army Group."

The 57th Wing's bombers continued flying missions to hit bridges and block the German retreat until the weather closed in on April 25. The 445th Squadron diarist, Captain Jackson, wrote: "'Going home' is the topic of the day. Everyone constantly talks or makes a ready listener for such talk. The war from this group's point of view is over. Targets change so fast that missions are uncertain from day to day."

The end of the war might have been in sight, but the enemy could still fight as hard as they did on the first day of the campaign. The 64th Fighter Squadron's James Dier came within moments of not completing his tour on one of his last missions, flown just a week before the war ended. By now an experienced pilot, Diers had become an element leader. He and his wingman were assigned an armed reconnaissance mission near Lake Garda in search of enemy transport. The main route that ran to the Brenner Pass was on the east side of the lake, and Diers recalled: "Flying over the lake, I noticed a large oil or gasoline tank truck stopped near the mouth of a tunnel." He was out of position to make a run at the truck and called on his wingman to attack it. "He claimed he couldn't see it, so I got into position and dived to strafe the truck, wondering why it hadn't taken cover in the tunnel opening. I soon found out. It was a trap, using the truck as bait!" Antiaircraft guns opened up at the P-47, firing from the tunnel, from the cliff above the tunnel, and from hillside positions to either side of the road. "I was flying almost at water level over the lake when I was hit. I called on my wingman to come down and help me but he said, 'They're shooting at you!' (As if I didn't know it) so I just radioed back, 'Let's get out of here!'"

Diers pushed his throttle forward to engage the P-47's emergency water injection system, which gave a 20 percent boost in horsepower. "The system was intended for just such a time as I was having. But it had one negative draw back – when used, it created a dark trail of smoke, which the German gunners saw and interpreted as evidence that they'd made a hit. They thus assumed that I was really damaged and so concentrated their fire. Black puffs of explosions surrounded me, but that wonderful P-47 roared on." Diers gradually gained altitude and found his wingman; he made it back home safely, "thanking the 'angel on my shoulder' once more."

Victory in Italy

As much as everyone expected the end, there was still time for more fighting and dying. The 321st Group flew its 895th mission to bomb the Cavarzere road bridge on April 25, led by Captain Wayne Kendall of the 445th Squadron in "Spirit of Portchester." The SHORAN-equipped B-25 "06," flown by Paul Young, led nine other bombers. The nine B-25s from the

Virtually every square inch of the Brenner Pass was covered by heavy antiaircraft guns. In March 1945, there were 517 heavy guns guarding the pass. This photo shows the location of the 14 Krupp 88s stationed at Rovereto. It was known as one of the hottest targets on the Brenner rail line. (57th Bomb Wing Archives, Edward Betts Collection)

P-47 DIVE-BOMBING

W.P. BOMBS ON GUN POSITIONS

TARGET

STAZ DI CERAINO RAIL FILL

This photo taken during the attack on the Staz Di Ceraino rail fill shows the various components of an attack. White phosphorus (W.P.) is dropped on the gun positions, while the P-47 escorts find targets to hit in the absence of enemy fighter threats, and the bombers brave the flak from 18 antiaircraft guns in the area. (57th Bomb Wing Archives, Edward Betts Collection)

446th Squadron included the veteran 43-4074, "27," flown by 1st Lieutenant Roland Jackson, which was among the first B-25Js the squadron had received a year earlier and was a survivor of 98 missions. Three bombers from the 447th Squadron rounded out the formation. The mission came under heavy fire from German flak. B-25J 43-4074, which had survived the battle of Cassino, the invasion of southern France, the first assault on the Gothic Line, and many missions during the battles over the Brenner, had an engine hit by flak and set on fire. Shrapnel from several explosions wounded bomb toggler Sergeant Robert Lattin, turret gunner Staff Sergeant Joseph Dalpos, radioman Sergeant Henry Nichols, and tail gunner Sergeant George W. Darnielle. Nichols, Dapos, and Darnielle bailed out. Darnielle's parachute failed to open and he fell to his death. Pilot Jackson kept the bomber in the air until they crossed the Allied lines, then crash-landed at the first airfield he spotted. The pilot and co-pilot managed to pull the wounded Sergeant Lattin out and ran from the burning bomber, which exploded minutes later.

Darnielle was the last member of the 57th Bomb Wing to be killed in action. Two other missions were flown that day by the 321st Group: they were "milk runs." Mission 897 proved to be the group's last mission of the war.

The same day that the 321st flew their final mission of the war, the Italian Committee of National Liberation called for a general uprising in the remaining German-held towns and cities across northern Italy. Genoa, Milan, and Turin were liberated by the partisans two days later.

Also on April 25, units of the Eighth Army advanced toward Venice and Trieste. On the Fifth Army front, units drove north toward Austria and northwest to Milan. On the left flank, the US 92nd Infantry Division advanced along the coast to Genoa. A rapid advance towards Turin by the Brazilian 1st Division took the German–Italian Army of Liguria by surprise, leading to its collapse and surrender.

On April 27, Benito Mussolini and his mistress, Clara Petacci, were stopped by communist partisans near the village of Dongo, on Lake Como, as they headed for Switzerland to board a plane and escape to Spain. They were taken to the village of Giulino di Mezzegra, where the next day they both were summarily executed, along with 15 other ministers and officials of the Italian Social Republic. On April 29, the bodies were trucked south to Milan and dumped on the old Piazza Loreto, which had been renamed "Piazza Quindici Martiri" in honor of 15 anti-fascists recently executed there. After being shot, kicked, and spat upon, the bodies were hung upside down on meat hooks from the roof of an Esso gas station and stoned by civilians.

On April 28, Captain Jackson wrote in the 445th Squadron's War Diary: "Well, it looks like the inevitable has happened, because without doubt, we have run out of targets. Today was a good flying day, but wing did not assign any targets and approved local transition flights. The battle lines are more fluid than ever before, and wherever our troops haven't entered, reports are that the Partisans are holding the towns. Milan, Turin and Venice were taken over by the Partisans and our forces moved up to make conjunction with them. It seems that the Allied command is reluctant to assign targets to us because of the possibility of assigned objectives already taken by rapidly moving ground forces. The day was climaxed with an announcement from General Clark that 'German resistance in Italy has virtually been eliminated.'"

By April 29, the German Army Group C had retreated on all fronts, having lost most of its fighting strength. General von Vietinghoff, who had stymied the Allied armies from Salerno to the Gothic Line, was left with little option but to surrender. That day, he signed the instrument of surrender on behalf of the German armies in Italy, with hostilities to come to a formal end on May 2. Upon hearing the news of the German surrender, Captain Jackson wrote: "After almost two-and-a-half years of slugging, bombing, mud and mountains, the enemy collapsed practically overnight and the Italian campaign closed in a blast of superlatives. We've made greater gains than any other theater; we've taken the biggest bag of prisoners on all fronts; we're the first theater to wind up; and we're the first theater to receive an unconditional surrender from an army group. As for the group, we just wound up our busiest month in existence and set a lot of records for future operations to aim at."

During the battle for the Brenner Pass, the 57th Bomb Wing flew 6,839 individual sorties between November 6, 1944, and April 6, 1945, in 380 missions. They dropped 10,267 tons of bombs on rail targets. In return, 46 B-25s were lost, while 532 were damaged; over 500 aircrew were killed or wounded.

Rail marshalling yards were often targeted by the 57th Bomb Wing. The resulting destruction was incredibly disruptive to the rail supply systems, as can be seen by this photo of the yards at Verona following an attack. (57th Bomb Wing Archives, Edward Betts Collection)

The 410ft Vignola road bridge across the Pamaro River was plastered by B-25s of the 321st Bomb Group on April 19, 1945, making it unusable for the retreating Wehrmacht forces. This bridge linked Highway 9 to the heavily defended area southwest of Bologna. (57th Bomb Wing Archives, Edward Betts Collection)

AFTERMATH

After the war, Captain Jack Valenti, a pilot with the 310th Bomb Group, General Robert Knapp, Commander of the 57th Bomb Wing, and General Ira Eaker, Commander of the USAAF in the Mediterranean, talk over old times. Some will remember Jack Valenti as the President of the Motion Picture Association of America and his appearance every year at the televised Academy Awards (Oscars) ceremony. (57th Bomb Wing Archives)

In June 1945, crews with sufficient seniority flew B-25s back to the United States while the rest of the men of the 57th Bomb Wing waited for ocean transport home. Among those who flew home was Captain Jack Valenti, veteran of 57 missions. He later recalled: "When I got back to Charleston, South Carolina, I landed, shut her down, climbed out, and got on my knees to kiss the ground. I promised myself I'd never fly another airplane again, and I never did." Twenty-five years later, as President of the Motion Picture Association of America, Valenti would take strong exception to the portrayal of the unit he served in and the friends he flew with in the movie *Catch-22*, based on the novel written by 340th Bomb Group bombardier Joseph Heller. Many other wing survivors also resented having their wartime careers detailed as they were in what has been called the greatest war novel of World War II. While Heller himself always maintained the work was "pure fiction," all of the events in the story can be traced to actual events in the 57th Wing during the final year of the war in Italy.

Mattox Photography
ALEXANDRIA, VIRGINIA

Dan Bowling returned to Los Angeles and married the girl who waited for him. The next year, he joined his father-in-law in forming a construction company that took advantage of the opportunities presented by the new GI Bill. Over the next 40 years, his company built nearly half the new homes in Torrance, Palos Verdes, and San Pedro, California. "After a year spent knocking down people's homes, I spent the rest of my life building homes," was the way he described his life. At his funeral in May 2016, held in the church he had built, three mourners remembered different occasions where they had witnessed Bowling give the coat off his back to a man who had none.

Paul Jackson returned to Indiana and took over the family farm. He never spoke of his experiences in the war until 2014, when his daughter Susan convinced him to attend that year's 57th Wing reunion. She later wrote, "After he reconnected with his old friends, he couldn't stop talking about what had happened and what they had done."

With hostilities ended, Colonel Anthony Hunter, Commander of the 310th Bombardment Group, gets a chance to inspect a Krupp 88mm flak battery and talk to the gun crews that caused so much grief, loss, and fear to the men in his command. (57th Bomb Wing Archives, Anthony Hunter Collection)

FURTHER READING

57th Bomb Wing Association, *The B-25 Over the Mediterranean, 50th Anniversary*, Creative Graphics (1992) (available online at http://57thbombwing.com/books.php)

57th Bomb Wing, *The Battle of the Brenner*, US Army Publication (1945) (available online at http://www.dansetzer.us/paper_index.htm)

Cleaver, Thomas McKelvey, *The Bridgebusters: The True Story of the Catch-22 Bomb Wing*, Regency Publishing (2016)

Hair, Charles A., *The Saga of 54 and More*, Robinson Typographics (1987)

Hair, Charles A., *Bullets, Bombs and Bridges: The Story of the 310th Bombardment Group, Part II*, Sawmill Graphics (2000)

Juglair, Roger, *Raid on the Settimo Road Bridges* (based on *Ponte San Martino: Maritirio di un paese valdostano*, Musumeci Editore (2008) (available online at http://www.dansetzer.us/Settimo.pdf)

Meder, Patricia Chapman, *The True Story of Catch 22*, Casemate (2012)

Military Intelligence Service, German Antiaircraft Artillery, War Department (1943) (available online at https://stephentaylorhistorian.files.wordpress.com/2020/02/german-aa-weapons.pdf)

Oyster, Harold E. & Esther, M., *The 319th in Action*, Burch Directory Co (1976)

Pace, Steve, *B-25 Mitchell Units of the MTO*, Osprey Publishing (2002)

Setzer, Dan, *Historical Sources for the Events in Joseph Heller's Novel, Catch-22*, Baltimore (2019) (available online at http://www.dansetzer.us/heller_index.htm)

Taddei, Dominique, *U.S.S. Corsica: L'île porte-avions*, Les éditions Albiana (2003)

Taddei, Dominique, *We 'Corsicans': Récits & Témoignages*, Les éditions Albiana (2016)

Additional online resources

57th Bomb Wing Association website: http://57thbombwing.com/

Fiction

Heller, Joseph, *Catch 22*, Simon & Schuster (1961)

INDEX

References to images are in **bold**.